The
BIG BOOK
of Ready-to-Use
THEME UNITS

by
Ellen Keller

SCHOLASTIC
PROFESSIONAL BOOKS

New York • Toronto • London • Auckland • Sydney

For Lola Kanneman,
my friend from the Minnesota days.
When it comes to creative teaching
and creative living,
she's the best.

Designed by Intergraphics
Production by Intergraphics
Cover design by Vincent Ceci
Cover illustration by Ajin
Illustrations by Don Robison
ISBN 0-590-49166-0

Contents

Continued

Part 3

**SPRING
111**

Introduction

The Big Book of Ready-to-Use Theme Units is devised as a tool for high-interest learning with a minimum of teaching preparation. The approach in all of the theme units is whole language instruction with an eye to teachers' valuable and limited time. The aim of the book is to provide fun learning activities across a variety of themes and curriculum areas. The activities are designed to tap students' prior knowlege, encourage research, and engage thinking skills.

○ **Books and/or other resources** for every unit are listed. For hands-on projects, there are no requirements for items such as a handsaw or fifty pounds of cement. The children can collect what are mostly regular school supplies or "junk" such as old food containers and newspapers.

○ **Fast Facts** are provided where appropriate, for talking specifically about subjects such as dinosaurs, weather, ants and frogs. With this information, you will be able to speak about specific questions which interest each child personally.

○ **Deciding which units to use and when** requires only a quick read. At the first or second grade level, certain activities can be scaled down. At the fourth grade level, the theme units have obvious built-in ideas for expansion. The seasonal listings in the Table of Contents are only suggestions. The unit on friendship might be best used in September. "Summer Vacation" might work best in June, while "Skeletons" seems a natural for Halloween-time. The choice is yours.

○ **All the units are self-contained.** However, parts or all of the units can be used with your prescribed curriculum and required texts. Some units, such as "Codes" or "Giants," provide a nice break during a gloomy fall or winter week. Themes such as these can entertain while still emphasizing the basics of reading, language arts, and other areas of your curriculum.

○ **Working and socializing in groups** provides the focus of some activities, and is also built into most projects. Much recent research has confirmed the importance of the child's emotional education, which includes learning how to relate to others, knowing that everyone has positive and negative feelings, learning how to work effectively and respectfully in groups, and how to get along at home and when sharing school and social lives. And so the activities in this book provide opportunities for students to work in whole-group and small-group settings, as well as individually. The values imbedded in the projects promote cooperation and respect for others.

○ **The themes are carried out through cross-curricular activities**. Each heading describes the subject, such as reading, language arts, social studies, or science. Note: not every unit contains activities for every curriculum area. However, activities can be inter-changed between units. For example, the information in the unit on Native Americans could have relevance in the unit on rocks and soil. The possibilities for exchange are here for you to use, adapt, and explore according to your needs and interests.

○ **The structure and format of the book has been kept deliberately loose.** You will notice that some units contain one activity sheet, others two. Some units are more detailed than others, but all contain plenty of suggestions for research and discovery. The purpose is to allow for purposeful, fun learning with lots of input from you and your students.

FALL

Friends

One of the best things about beginning a school year is discovering new friends and renewing old friendships. The activities in this unit can help children see that they are already adept at making and keeping friends. In reflecting on their own friendships, they will explore what it means to have a friend, and to be a friend. They will also learn the value of friendship and the role friendship plays in creating a positive and supportive atmosphere in the classroom.

▷ Getting Started

Ask students to think about the people who are their friends. Encourage them to recall all the details they can about adventures, fun times, and even troubles they may have shared with their friends. Distribute long strips of paper (adding-machine paper works well), one to each student, along with crayons or markers and invite students to start their time lines with the first memory of meeting their friend. They can then chronicle their shared adventures, etc.. The time lines can be decorated, illustrated, and shared by being read aloud to the class before being displayed on a "Friendship Bulletin Board."

▽ Word Map

Creating a Community of Friends

The time line activity will probably point out that although each of the children has some special friend, somewhere, not all children have special friends within the class. In order to encourage group spirit and friendship in the classroom, write the word "Friends" in large letters on the chalkboard, and help the students create a word map around it.

Then allow children to work in pairs or groups to create words or pictures for a bulletin board display. The may want to draw graffiti-style letters, cut letters out of colored paper, or use ready-made alphabet letters from your supply of classroom decorations. They may want to illustrate the board with photos of themselves brought from home, pictures from magazines or

newspapers, or their own artwork. The important thing is to allow them as much ownership of the project as possible, while remaining under your guidance, so that it truly is a cooperative, empowering activity which will give the students a feeling of friendship and belonging.

Reading

Suggested Books About Friendship

Anna's Secret Friend by Yoriko Tsutsui (Viking)

Everett Anderson's New Friend by Lucille Clifton (Holt, Rinehart, & Winston)

Friends by Helen Heine (Atheneum)

It's Not Fair by Charlotte Zolotow (Harper & Row)

B-e-s-t Friends by Patricia Reilly Giff (Dell)

Bunk Mates by Joanna Hurwitz (Scholastic)

Nothing's Fair in Fifth Grade by Barth De Clements (Scholastic)

Miracle at the Plate by Matt Christopher (Little, Brown)

Writing

Friendship Story Maps

The children can choose a book about friendship, and after reading it, make a book map. They can then share their book maps and tell why others will want to read the book.

Sample book map format:

Book Title:
The most important things happened in this order:
1.
2.
3.

What this story says about friendship:

Language Arts

Talking and Listening

Discuss with the children the importance of talking and listening in friendship. Invite the children to talk about how they feel when one person always does all the talking, or when a friend won't talk at all, or won't listen.

The children can then take the Top Secret Self-Test for Friendship on page 12. Emphasize that the purpose of this test is to help individuals to think over ideas about friendship by themselves. Encourage children to talk about points on the test they feel comfortable discussing. Help them think of ways to use the test to be a better friend.

 ## Creative Dramatics

Making Up Friendship Plays

In groups of three or four, the students can discuss, plan, practice, write, and present short plays in which friendship is an underlying theme. If some students have difficulty in thinking of ideas, suggest one of these:

○ Your best friend since nursery school met a new friend two weeks ago. You and your friend used to do everything together, but now your friend has no time for you—and the new person is getting all of your old friend's attention.
○ You have two good friends, and love to play with both of them, but there's one problem: neither one can stand the other! You plan a way to get them together.
○ Someone new comes into the class and seems very shy.

 ## Physical Education

Cooperative Playground Olympics

Talk about two friends working together to achieve something that involves planning, considering each other's strengths and weaknesses, and encouraging a positive attitude in each other. Then help children organize "Playground Olympics," with sack, relay, running, wheelbarrow, backward running or any other events in which students must work as partners for success.

Reading and Writing

Friendship Mini-Books

Make and distribute copies of the mini book pattern on page 13.

Directions for making the Friendship Mini Book:

Students should:
1. Cut on the dotted lines.
2. Stack the pages together, title page on top, and staple the pages together at the upper left-hand corner.
3. Have students write and illustrate their friendship stories on the blank pages.

The Top-Secret Self-Test for Being a Good Friend

Read and answer the questions. Your answers can be a secret if you want them to be. It's up to you. Put a check in front of everything you think is true.

Part 1. About Me

☐ I wish I had more friends.

☐ I am absolutely perfect. I never do anything wrong.

☐ I like whining. It makes people do what I want.

☐ I think I should always play what others want to play.

☐ I ask others if I can join when I want to play.

☐ I wait around for someone to invite me to play with them.

Part 2. About Others

☐ You can tell right away if you want to be friends with another person.

☐ You can't give someone another chance if they don't play fair.

☐ If someone comes to my house, I get to decide everything about what we do.

☐ Getting mad will make others do what you want to do.

Friendship Mini-Book

1. Cut on the dotted lines and put the pages in order.
2. Staple the pages in order.
3. Use the blank spaces and lines to draw and write a story about you and your friend.

_____
(friend's name)
**and Me
And How We Became Friends
by**
_____
(your name)

1.

The first time I met
_____
(friend's name)

2.

We _____

_____

_____

3.

_____

_____

_____

. . . And we both lived happily
ever after.

4.

Ants

If your students have never studied ants before, they (and you) are in for something special. Ants have jobs, are hardworking, help each other, can construct walls, and even (sometimes) go to war! An investigation of ants will fascinate your students and will also help them appreciate these tiny, yet terrific creatures.

Fast Facts

○ Some insects live all their lives in isolation, but ants live in social units called colonies. They may live in mounds of earth, in tree trunks, under flat rocks, under the sidewalk, or in abandoned termite nests.

○ There are many kinds of ants, including Carpenter, Weaver, Honey, and Army ants.

○ Each kind can be divided into three types: winged males, female workers, and one queen per colony.

○ Ants hibernate in winter, sleeping in a big ball around their queen. They walk in their sleep so that the ants on the outside of the ball can take turns moving to the inside for warmth.

○ Your students would probably not want to eat like ants. Worker ants forage for dead insects and sweet things. They chew these up and bring them to the queen, the baby ants, and other workers who are busy cleaning the nest or building tunnels. They regurgitate the food for the other members of the colony.

▷ Getting Started

Start your ant discussion, and get a laugh, by telling a joke. (Something like: "Guess what . . . I'm related to an insect. I have an 'ant'!") Mention the difference in spelling between human and insect "ants," and tell the class that they will be spending some time learning more about these interesting insects.

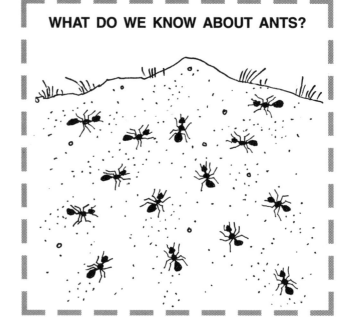

WHAT DO WE KNOW ABOUT ANTS?

▼ Reading

Some books that will help in the ant investigations are:

An Ant Colony, Heiderose and Fisher-Nagel (Carolrhoda)

Bugs, Parker and Wright (Greenwillow)

A First Look at Insects, Selsam and Hunt (Walker)

The Story of Ants, Shuttlesworth (Doubleday)

▼ Science

Exploring Ant Life

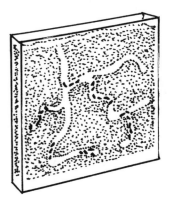

In order to help your students observe ants in action, you may want to buy an ant farm. (However, it will not contain a queen, so the colony will not be self-perpetuating.) Write to or call Museum Products, 84 Route 27, Mystic, CT 06355 (1-800-395-5400).

After your students have had a chance to observe the ants, make copies of the activity sheet on page 17. Read and discuss it with the class before inviting students to work alone or in pairs to use it to record the results of their ant investigations.

▼ Reading and Writing

Ant Fiction

Read to the children the picture book, *Two Bad Ants* by Chris Van Allsburg (Houghton, Mifflin). Read the story to the class without showing them the pictures, and tell them it's a mystery for them to figure out. Encourage them to listen carefully to learn what the ants find and what happens to them. After discussing the story, re-read it, this time showing the pictures. Invite the children to point out the real ant facts the author used. They can then write their own stories, using true ant facts.

▼ Language Arts

Light and Shadow Show

Invite children to create a play with talking ants as characters. Use the ant illustration on the activity sheet on page 17 as a pattern, and have the children copy it onto heavy paper. After copying the ant drawing, have the children cut it out and attach it with glue or tape to the end of a pencil in order to use it as a puppet.

By using a flashlight with a bright beam, and darkening the room, you can help children stage their plays as light-and-shadow shows on a blank wall.

▼ Music

New Lyrics to an Old Tune

Encourage students to write ant-themed new lyrics to the tune, "When Johnny Comes Marching Home Again." The new song can be called "The Ants Go Marching One by One," and students should be encouraged to use their imaginations to make the new song as funny and silly as possible.

✓ Language Arts

Homonym Fun

Refer to the joke you made about having an "ant" that started the unit. Discuss other words that sound alike but that are spelled differently and mean different things, like *bear* and *bare*, *pail* and *pale*, *tail* and *tale*, etc. Encourage students to make lists of all the homonyms they can think of, which they can post on a bulletin board, under the heading "Homonym Center." Allow them to continue to add more pairs of homonyms over time. When they have listed as many as they can think of, invite them to create stories, poems, or songs using the words on the list. (Suggested titles: "The Three Little Pears," "The Tale of a Pail," "As I Rode Down the Road." Your students are sure to come up with many others.)

✓ Math

Adding Ants (Subtracting, Too)

Have students create ant word problems. Provide them with blank sheets of paper on which to write the problems, and encourage them to illustrate them with funny drawings. Start them off with these suggestions:

○ The queen starts out alone.
○ She has twelve eggs.
○ She gets hungry and eats four.
○ Five of the eggs don't hatch.
○ The rest grow into workers.
○ How many workers are there?
○ The queen has eight more eggs.
○ How many ants are there now?

✓ Math

"As Strong as an Ant"

Ants can often be seen moving grains of dirt, or carrying bits of food back to their colonies. Sometimes the things they carry are bigger than they are—in fact, depending on the type of ant, most ants are able to carry objects that weigh ten to fifty times as much as the ant itself! (In comparison, a human is considered very strong if he or she can lift two or three times his or her own weight.) Bring in a scale and have students weigh themselves. When they have recorded their weights, ask them:

"How much weight could you lift if you were as strong as an ant? (A fifty pound child could lift an object weighing from five hundred to twenty-five hundred pounds.) Invite students to research the weights of objects like refrigerators, cars, etc., to find out how many of each item they could lift if they were as strong as an ant. Chart the information on a bulletin board.

Name: _____

Follow the Ants

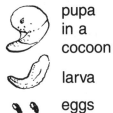
pupa
in a
cocoon

larva

eggs

Choose one ant to observe. Watch carefully to see what it does. Does it look like the picture at the top of this page? _____

Put salt, sugar, bread crumbs, pieces of paper, or anything else you can think of, in front of the ant. (Be sure not to hurt it!)

Watch what the ant does with the different things you put in its path, then use this activity sheet to write down what you see.

Things I put in front of the ant:	What the ant did:

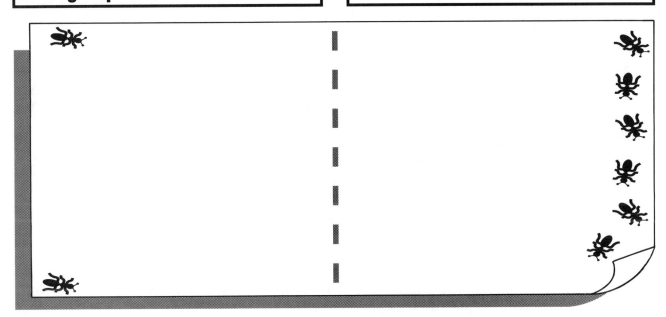

Did the ant seem to like any of the things? Did it seem to dislike any? What do you think about ants now? Use the space below to write your opinion.

_____

_____

_____

_____

Dinosaurs

"Dinosaurs" is one of those subjects that children readily embrace with enthusiasm. Indeed, your students may already have a great deal of information about dinosaurs. Take an opportunity to build on what they already know by providing them with a truly useful and satisfying experience in researching new information.

 Fast Facts

❍ Dinosaurs were the most successful group of land animals ever to roam the earth. They dominated our planet for over 150 million years. In fact, they existed over such a long period of time, that the last dinosaurs existed closer in time to *us* than they did to their first dinosaur ancestors!

❍ Paleontology is the study of fossils. (Since there are no dinosaurs living today, scientists must study fossils to find out about dinosaurs.)

❍ Sauropod dinosaurs (such as Diplodocus, Apatosaurus, and Brachiosaurus) were the biggest animals ever to roam the land. These gigantic creatures were all slow-moving, with small brains. They were plant eaters and walked on all fours. As big as they were, however, they are probably not the biggest animals *ever*: The blue whale, which exists today, is the record-holder (at 200 tons, compared to *only* 77 tons for the brachiosaurus.

❍ The creature that used to be called Brontosaurus was the result of a paleontological mixup: its discoverer mixed up its bones with another dinosaur called Camarasaurus. The correct name for the creature we knew as Brontosaurus is Apatosaurus (deceptive lizard).

❍ Most dinosaur names are Greek (e.g. "Triceratops" means three-horned-face—from *tri* [three]; *cera* [horn]; *tops* [face].)

Saurus means lizard and *don* means tooth. Some dinosaurs are named for the places in which their fossilized remains were found (Albertosaurus, for example, means "lizard found in Alberta.")

 Getting Started

To start this unit, put up a large sheet of paper on which children can write or dictate known dinosaur information. On subsequent days during the theme unit study, they can add to this list by writing in different colors so that they can see how their information is increasing. For example:

▼ Science

Making A Dinosaur Information Bulletin Board

Back a bulletin board with paper and copy the chart below. Print the names of the three Periods within the Mesozoic Era and some names of dinosaurs.

Depending on the abilities and interests of your group, choose some of the following points for discussion and activities.

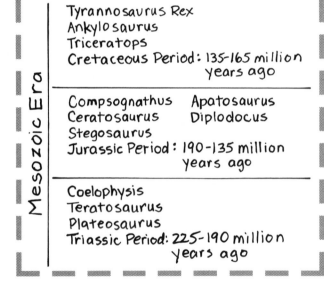

Mesozoic Era	Tyrannosaurus Rex Ankylosaurus Triceratops Cretaceous Period: 135-165 million years ago
	Compsognathus Apatosaurus Ceratosaurus Diplodocus Stegosaurus Jurassic Period: 190-135 million years ago
	Coelophysis Teratosaurus Plateosaurus Triassic Period: 225-190 million years ago

○ The Mesozoic Era is only one of the three divisions of the Phanerozoic eon of the earth's history. The others are the Paleozoic and the Cenozoic. Challenge students to figure out which period humans belong to. (Humans belong to the Zenozoic—which means "recent life." Paleozoic means "ancient life" and the Mesozoic means "middle life.")

○ Point out that the oldest period, the Triassic, is down at the bottom of the chart, because the earliest dinosaur fossils were found deepest down in the ground.

After millions of years, the rocks and soil of the Triassic Period were covered with the rocks and soil of the Jurassic Period, during which new kinds of dinosaurs lived. The Cretaceous Period was the last for dinosaurs, and it produced the biggest ones.

○ Ask the children to identify any familiar dinosaur names listed on the bulletin board. Some children will welcome these new "big words" to add to their information about dinosaurs.

○ In pairs, children can search resources for pictures of dinosaurs listed on the bulletin board. Volunteers can sketch dinosaur pictures in their appropriate periods.

▽ Reading

Looking Up Dinosaur Pictures and Information

Reproduce this list and send children to the library to find these and other books. Display them in a classroom "Dino-Center".

The Dinosaur Fun Book by Gillian Osband (Scholastic)

Dinosaurs and How They Lived by Steve Parker (Dorling Kindersley)

Dinosaur Story by Joanna Cole (Scholastic)

Dinosaurs and More Dinosaurs by M. Jean Craig (Scholastic)

Dinosaur Dig: Cooperative Game in a Book by Liza Schafer (Scholastic)

Giant Dinosaurs by Peter Dodson and Peter Lerangis (Scholastic)

Giant Dinosaurs by Erna Rowe (Scholastic)

How Did Dinosaurs Live? by Kunhiki Hisa (Lerner)

Let's Go Dinosaur Tracking by Miriam Schlein (HarperCollins)

Living With Dinosaurs by Patricia Lauber (Bradbury Press)

If Dinosaurs Came to Town by Dom Mansell (Little, Brown)

The Macmillan Book of Dinosaurs and Other Prehistoric Creatures by Mary Elting (Macmillan)

The Smallest Dinosaurs by Seymour Simon (Crown)

Strange Creatures That Really Lived by Millicent Selsam (Scholastic)

▽ Social Studies

Conserving Natural Resources

Children may be surprised to learn that dinosaurs are useful to humans today—their remains are one of the ingredients of "fossil fuels," such as petroleum, which are derived from the decomposed remains of plants and animals that lived millions of years ago. Buried deep inside the earth, high pressure and temperatures converted them into the hydrocarbon fuels we use today for heating and transportation.

Challenge children to list reasons why humans must think of ways to save these fossil fuels (Possible answers: there are no more dinosaurs around to create more fuel, and even if there were, it takes millions of years to create it, and we'd have run out by then; fossil fuels are sources of pollution, etc.) Invite interested volunteers to research alternative energy sources and report their findings to the class.

▽ Science

Forming Fossils

Students may not realize that all we know about dinosaurs we've learned from fossils. *The Dinosaur Encyclopedia* by Dr. Michael Benton (Simon and Schuster) is a good resource for teaching about the fossilization process. *Dinosaurs and How They Lived* by Steve Parker (Dorling Kindersley) is another excellent resource for younger or less able readers. After discussing fossils and

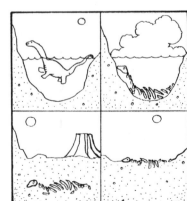

fossilization with your students, you may want to arrange a class trip to a museum with a dinosaur exhibit. (Partial listing follows.) Reproduce and distribute copies of page 22 and help students complete it individually. Student diagrams should look something like the illustration on page 20.

Field Trip

Taking your class to a natural history museum is a fun way to begin, conclude, extend, or enrich your Dinosaur unit.

Dinosaur Museums

United States

Museum of Northern Arizona, Flagstaff, Arizona
Los Angeles Museum of Natural History, Los Angeles, California
Peabody Museum of Natural History, New Haven, Connecticut
Denver Museum of Natural History, Denver, Colorado
Field Museum of Natural History, Chicago, Illinois
Museum of Comparative Zoology, Cambridge, Massachusetts
Museum of Natural History, Princeton, New Jersey
Ghost Ranch, Abiquiu, New Mexico
American Museum of Natural History, New York City, New York
Dinosaur Valley State Park, Glen Rose, Texas
Dinosaur National Monument, Jensen, Utah
National Museum of Natural History, Smithsonian Institution, Washington, D.C.

Science

Designing A Dinosaur Habitat

Children can pair up to look in books for pictures of the earth's surface during one of the three periods in the Mesozoic Era. They can then use a cardboard box, clay, cut paper, and random junk to create a habitat for toy dinosaurs they bring from home. After completing the habitat, they can set up their dinosaurs in it and give a little talk to the group, showing what they know about this particular period and the dinosaurs who lived then.

Math

Visualizing the Size of Dinosaurs

Help children discover how they'd stack up in proportion to the dinosaurs. Measure the heights of several student volunteers, and write the information on the chalkboard.

Then invite students to look up the actual heights of several of their favorite dinosaurs; and write those numbers on the board, along with the dinosaurs' names.

Challenge students to find out how many of them would have to stand on each other's shoulders to be able to look a Tyrannosaurus Rex in the eye. Or, tell students that their heights can be used as units of measurement. Point out that, for example, "Matthew is four feet tall, so we can call a four-foot-tall measurement one 'Matthew'." If a Brachiosaurus was forty feet tall, how many 'Matthews' tall is a Brachiosaurus?" (10). Invite students to create their own word problems involving themselves and dinosaurs.

Forming Fossils

Dinosaur fossils may be footprints in rock, or skeletons. The numbered sentences in the boxes below show the steps in the process of fossilization when a dinosaur has died and fallen into a river or a lake. Draw a picture in each of the boxes that shows what's happening.

1. The dinosaur dies and his body sinks to the bottom of a lake or river.

2. After a long time, the flesh is eaten (or rots) and the skeleton is covered by sand or mud.

3. More time passes. The mud and sand turn into rock. After millions of years, the river bed may now be dry land, and the mud and sand have turned to rock.

4. As more time passes, the rock is worn away by rain and wind, and the dinosaur skeleton can be seen. Paleontologists may find it.

Codes and Secrets

What is a code? Children may suggest that a code is a message in which unusually-arranged letters, numbers, or other symbols are used to convey secrets. Encourage children to share experiences they have had with codes—either learning them or trying to crack them. Does anyone in your class know a secret language? Ask them for a demonstration.

 Getting Started

Copy and distribute the activity sheet on page 26. Tell children that aside from allowing one to learn secret information, inventing and cracking codes develops problem-solving skills, increases concentration, and improves spelling. Give them time to crack the codes on each line of the sheet. Afterwards, allow children to discuss their solutions and tell how they arrived at them.

FINDTHESECRETCODEBOX.
FIND THE SECRET CODE BOX.

TH EB OX IS HI DD EN IN TH EP AR K
THE BOX IS HIDDEN IN THE PARK.

KLAW OT EHT YEKNOM EGAC.
WALK TO THE MONKEY CAGE.

6-9-14-4   20-8-5   2-21-19-8   2-25   20-8-5
6-12-1-7   16-15-12-5.
20-8-5   2-15-24   9-19   21-14-4-5-18   9-20.
FIND THE BUSH BY THE FLAG POLE.
THE BOX IS UNDER IT.

 Language Arts

Working With Secret Code Partners at Home

Ask children if there is someone at home—a brother, a sister, a parent, or a relative—who might enjoy receiving and sending secret messages. Suggest to children that they leave messages in code for that person on the refrigerator door, behind a chair, in a book, in a secret drawer, or under a pillow. Their secret-message partner can attempt to decode the message, write one for them in the same language, and leave it in the designated spot. Children and their partners can take turns inventing and cracking codes. Ask children who try this activity to share their experiences (and maybe their messages!) with the class.

 **Writing**

Decoding Messages from the Secret Message Box

Set up a secret message box in your classroom. In private, ask several children each day to put secret messages in the box, along with their code-names. Children can use any of the codes from the activity sheet, or they can invent their own. Have an equal number of volunteers each day pick up the messages from the box and try to decode them.

Decoders must try to crack the code and guess who sent the messages. If they cannot, the messages go back into the box. Message-writers who are able to keep their identities a secret for a week can receive a Master Secret Coder Award designed by a group appointed for that purpose.

 **Reading**

Reading Books about Codes and Secret Messages

Children interested in further reading on the subject of codes and secret messages will enjoy reading the following books.

Code Books

Code Buster by Burton Albert, Jr. (Albert Whitman)

How to Keep a Secret: Writing and Talking in Code by E. James and C. Barkin (Lothrop, Lee & Shepard Company)

How to Write Codes and Send Secret Messages by John Peterson (Scholastic)

 Social Studies

Using a Civil War Code

The activity sheet on page 27 presents an actual secret code used during the Civil War. Ask children to tell something they know about the Civil War, and write their ideas on the chalkboard. You may wish to fill in the following points:

○ The Civil War was fought during the years 1861–1865, when Abraham Lincoln was President.
○ The war took place between the North—called the Union—and the South—called the Confederacy.
○ The immediate cause of the war was the Confederacy's wish to separate from the United States and form its own country.
○ The central issue dividing North and South was the South's widespread use of slave labor to support its plantation economy.
○ After a bloody war, the Confederacy surrendered, the practice of slavery was abolished, and the United States remained intact.

Go over the activity sheet with children and ask them to use the key to figure out the message.

Message
MEET ME AT THE SWAMP.

◥ Social Studies

Researching Codes

List the following types of codes on the chalkboard and encourage children to add to the list:

- ○ sound signals (Morse Code)
- ○ spoken codes (Pig Latin, Egg, Opp)
- ○ secret passwords
- ○ acronyms
- ○ word substitution
- ○ light signals (for nautical and aeronautic use)
- ○ flag signals (for nautical and aeronautic use)

Then have pairs or small groups of children choose one of these codes and research its origin, history, and use. If possible, have children give a demonstration of the code.

◥ Math

Writing Number Codes

Use addition, subtraction, multiplication, division, or any math process your group is working on as a basis for writing secret messages. Assign the letter A to the number 1, the letter B to the number 2, and so on. Have children write math problems in which the answers serve as the letters of the message. For example, the message "KEEP OUT" can be figured out by answering the following addition and subtraction problems: 4 + 7 (11 = K); 21 − 16 (5 = E); 15 − 10 (5 = E); 9 + 7 (16 = P); 32 − 17 (15 = O); 13 + 8 (21 = U); 90 − 70 (20 = T).

Cracking Codes

Are you a good code cracker? Crack these codes to find out!
There is a different code for every line.

FINDTHESECRETCODEBOX.

_____

TH EB OX IS HI DD EN IN TH EP AR K

_____

KLAW OT EHT YEKNOM EGAC.

_____

6-9-14-4　　20-8-5　　2-21-19-8　　2-25　　20-8-5
6-12-1-7　　16-15-12-5.
20-8-5　　2-15-24　　9-19　　21-14-4-5-18　　9-20.

_____

_____

_____

A Symbol Code

One name for the key below is the Civil War Cipher. Use the key and figure out the message.

Key:

Message:

Use the key. Write your own message. Ask a friend to read it.

_____

_____

_____

_____

_____

_____

The Moon

For many children, the moon in the night sky is an object of wonder, beauty, and mystery. In this unit, students will explore their own responses to the moon and begin to absorb some moon science.

 Getting Started

Use the following book titles to launch your moon unit.
Have children listen and then respond to the plot, humor, and characters' understandings of moon concepts as presented in each book:

Mooncake by Frank Asch (Scholastic)

Happy Birthday, Moon by Frank Asch (Simon and Schuster)

Many Moons by James Thurber (Harcourt Brace Jovanovich)

 Science

Moon Questions and Answers

Ask the children to dictate statements and questions about the moon. Record their information beneath one of the two following column headings printed on a large piece of chart paper:

What We Know About the Moon	What We Would Like to Know About the Moon

Each day refer to the chart. To the first column continue to add information as it is learned. In the second column, ask students to point out and cross off any questions about the moon that are answered.

 Reading and Math

Charting Moon Reading

Help the children search out library books and magazines featuring stories or articles about the moon. Then, create a bar graph reflecting student responses to what they have read. On a bulletin board covered with craft paper draw enough vertical lines to create one column for each student. Provide students with index cards, fine line markers and cellophane tape.

As each student reads a moon selection, he or she prints the title of the selection on the front of the card and uses tape to fasten the card "hinge-style" to the board in the column above his or her name. The student then lifts the card up and records a brief response to the reading (e.g., "I liked this book because it had neat moon photographs."). Encourage students to be as specific as possible, and allow students class time to share their responses with the group.

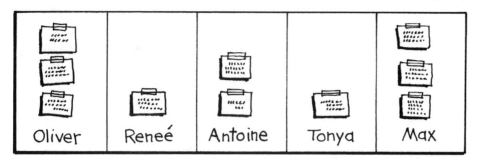

Oliver	Reneé	Antoine	Tonya	Max

▽ Language Arts

Writing A Moon Adventure

Have children scan their moon resources in order to make a list of moon words and phrases such as: moonbeam, man in the moon, harvest moon, moon dust, full moon, etc.

Provide each child with a copy of the activity sheet on page 31 and read the verse printed there together. Have children fill in the first two blank spaces in the verse with words and phrases from the list (or with any other nouns they may choose) and then complete the story as they wish. Have students illustrate their work and staple both writing and illustrations to large sheets of construction paper for display.

▽ Reading and Science

Observing the Moon's Changing Shape

Read *Moon Man* by Tomi Ungerer (Delacorte) and *The Moon Seems to Change* by Franklyn M. Branley (Harper Trophy Books) aloud. Ask the children to respond to each one.

Ask the children to observe the night sky for two or three nights, and report what they saw, and recall other moon shapes they've seen. In order for the children to understand that the moon does not really change shape, set up the experiment as shown in the illustration.

Art

Building a Lunar Space Station

Tell your children that in their lifetime the United States will probably build a space station on the moon. Have students talk about how the station would have to replicate the conditions on earth and how that might be done. Have children locate picture books and magazine articles about space stations. They or you can read interesting parts while others point out details in the pictures.

Help your class create a lunar station play space using a large appliance box. Paint the box silver or grey and use letter and number stencils to paint labels onto the outside walls. On the inside of the station, have students paint a control panel. Supply realistic-looking control panel buttons and dials (made from glued-on plastic bottle caps and margarine tub tops secured with large brass fasteners). Complete your lunar module with cut-out windows covered with colorful cellophane.

Listening and Speaking

Understanding Poetic Images

Read aloud the following passage from "The Highwayman" by Alfred Noyes:
"The wind was a torrent of darkness among the gusty trees,
The moon was a ghostly galleon tossed upon cloudy seas,
The road was a ribbon of moonlight over the purple moor,
And the highwayman came riding-riding-riding-
The highwayman came riding, up to the old inn-door."

Explain that a "galleon" is a big sailing ship used on the seas hundreds of years ago. Have the children explain why the poet decided to compare the moon to a galleon, then, invite the class to brainstorm additional "Moon Similies." Record these on a large piece of chart paper and post the chart in your writing center for students wishing to incorporate such lunar imagery in their own writing.

Writing

Sending Away for Information

Some children may wish to write to NASA at the following address for up-to-the-minute information about current space projects:
NASA Educational Briefs
National Aeronautics and
Space Administration
Washington, D.C. 20546

A Moon Adventure

Fill in the blanks to create your own moon adventure, then draw a picture to illustrate your story in the space below.

The man in the moon is talking to me,
"Come up, come up, come up," says he.
So I go up and guess what I see?

A _____ and a _____
are looking at me.
And then _____

_____

_____

_____

_____

_____

Money

Some educators seem to feel that classroom discussions focusing on money will instill questionable values in children and lead them to the belief that money equals happiness. On the contrary, an appreciation of the real value of money—how to save it, how to earn it, and how to use it to its best advantage—is a valuable learning experience for children who will one day grow up to be responsible and independent people.

 Getting Started

In order to assess students' understanding of the value of money—which will probably vary widely from child to child—ask them to fill out the questionnaire on the activity sheet on page 35. Then go over the questionnaire and discuss children's responses. (In leading your discussion it is important to consider the range of ethnic and economic backgrounds from which the children come, and to tailor the discussion accordingly.) You may want to save the questionnaires for the end of the unit in order to give children the opportunity to evaluate their increased understanding of the subject.

 Social Studies

Going on a Comparison Shopping Trip

Lead a discussion on what it means to comparison shop. Point out that when shopping it is important to compare unit prices of several competing brands. Advise children against buying the first thing they see—or the brand that looks the best on TV—as they will often not be getting the most for their money.

Take children on a shopping trip to a supermarket or a mall. Divide the class into pairs. Have each pair choose a type of item to buy—breakfast cereal, cleanser, spaghetti sauce, or paper towels are good choices. Encourage them to compare prices and quantities and to take notes. When they are back in the classroom, ask children to share their experiences and respond to questions such as these:

❍ Which item would you buy? Why?
❍ How did you make your choice?
❍ What was the most surprising thing you found out?
❍ Why is it *not* a good idea to buy the first thing you see?
❍ How could you save money by comparison shopping?
❍ How might this experience be useful to you in the future?

Note: As an alternative, if going out to shop is unfeasible, comparison-shop through newspaper ads.

 ## Language Arts

Making A Personal Spending/Savings Book

Suggest that children make personal spending/savings books to keep track of the money they get, save, and spend each week. To make the book, children can tie or staple together several sheets of drawing paper and create sections such as "My Weekly Budget," "Ways to Make Money," "Ideas for Saving Money," and "Things to Save Up For."

 ## Reading

Looking For Money Management Ideas

Good Cents: Every Kid's Guide to Making Money by Elizabeth Wilkinson (Little, Brown)

The Money Book: A Smart Kid's Guide to Savvy Saving and Spending by Elaine Wyatt and Stan Hinden (Tambourine Books)

 ## Writing

The Greedy Kid Tale

Tell children that many folk tales and stories from around the world have as their themes people who are punished for their selfishness and greed. Ask children if they know any of these stories. (They may suggest "The Fisherman and His Wife" or "The Three Wishes.") Then suggest that children write their own tales called "The Greediest Kid in the World." As a prewriting activity, encourage children to respond to questions such as these and to jot down their answers:

❍ Where does the greediest kid in the world live? An apartment building? Farm? Desert? House by a mall?
❍ How does the greediest kid get what he/she wants? By whining? Throwing tantrums? Getting angry? Bribery?
❍ What is the greediest thing the greediest kid ever did?
❍ What event changed the greediest kid? How did he/she change?

Encourage children to write the first drafts of their stories and read them to a partner. After the drafts are revised, allow time for children to read them to the class.

Art

Make a "Smart Shopping" Poster

Start off your discussion on what it means to be a "smart shopper" by asking children if they think about the following before they buy a particular item:

❍ Do I really need what I'm buying?
❍ Am I buying too much food because I am hungry?
❍ How long will I use it before I get tired of it or it breaks?
❍ Can I get the product for a better price if I choose another brand?
❍ Can I get the same product for a better price at another store?

○ What can labels tell me that would help me to decide if one product is a better buy than another?

After the discussion, encourage children to make and illustrate posters depicting the shopping tips they feel are most important. You may want to suggest a poster with a "Do" and a "Don't" side.

 Art

Making the Best Bank Ever

Children will enjoy designing and creating their own banks. Have children collect used plastic bottles from soda, detergent, or bleach and advise them to clean the bottles thoroughly. Then ask them to think of a way to decorate the bottles for use as a bank. Here are some suggestions for things to think about:

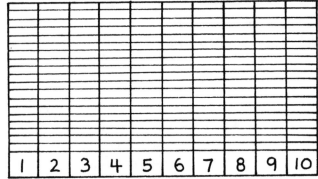

1. Look at the shape of the bottle. Could you make it resemble an animal, a person, or a cartoon figure?
2. What can you tie, glue, or paint on the bottle to make the bank special?
3. Can you think of a funny name for the bank?
4. How can you put money into the bank and take it out?

After children complete their banks, encourage them to display them to the class and discuss how they will use them.

 Math

Charting the Results of a Survey

On the chalkboard, draw a bar graph outline like the one shown. There should be 10 columns, one for each question on the activity sheet on page 36. The number of spaces in each column should be the number of children present in the room that day.

Tell children that a survey is a collection of responses to a question or series of questions, designed to show how a particular group feels about a certain issue or issues. Emphasize that in a survey there are no right or wrong answers. Invite children to answer the questions on the activity sheet. Then have children draw a graph like the one on the chalkboard. Find out how many children answered "yes" to Question 1 on the survey and color in the same number of spaces in the corresponding column on the graph. Have children color their graphs in the same way. Continue with the rest of the questions until all columns on the graphs are colored.

Ask children to read from their own graphs to answer these questions about their classmates' responses to the questionnaire.

○ To which questions did most of the children in the class answer "yes"? What does this tell you?
○ To which questions did the fewest number of children in the class answer "yes"? What does this tell you?
○ Is there a right or a wrong answer to questions on a survey? What exactly is an opinion?

Name: _____

Money Questionnaire

Write **yes** or **no**.

1. People make money at work by printing it. _____

2. You can go to any bank. They will give you money. _____

3. My family could live for a month on $100. _____

4. A bike costs the same in every store. _____

5. Milk costs the same in every store. _____

6. I would give up treats to save for something like a bike or something else I wanted badly. _____

7. When I have kids I will give them more money than my parents give me. _____

Can you explain what the following sentences mean?

1. I know how to stretch my money.

_____

_____

_____

2. Money grows in a savings account in the bank.

_____

_____

_____

3. People do not keep all the money they make. They must pay taxes to the government for services.

_____

_____

_____

Allowance Questionnaire

Write **yes** or **no.**

1. Every girl and boy should get an allowance. _____

2. You should do chores to get an allowance. _____

3. Parents can decide how much the allowance will be. _____

4. Kids should make their own money through work. _____

5. Part of an allowance should be saved. _____

6. Presents should be bought with an allowance. _____

7. Food treats should come from an allowance. _____

8. Giving to charity should come from an allowance. _____

9. You should be able to get an advance on an allowance for something special. _____

10. The amount of an allowance should be raised every year. _____

Native Americans

Interest, understanding, and respect for Native Americans can be fostered through the study of one tribe, one aspect of tribal life, or an overview of the vast numbers of tribes and their lifestyles.

 Fast Facts

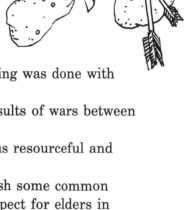

○ Native Americans lived in North and South America many years before Europeans came to these lands.
○ Native Americans never named themselves *Indians*. Rather, they used the names of their nations and the separate tribes within them.
○ Native Americans introduced the world to important, life-saving foods such as potatoes and corn. They also introduced tobacco.
○ Before the Europeans came, Native Americans had no firearms or horses. All movement was done on foot. Hunting was done with tools such as bows and arrows.
○ Controversy continues about the causes, purposes, and results of wars between the new settlers and Native Americans.
○ Pre-colonial family and tribal life for Native Americans was resourceful and nurturing as well as difficult.
○ Despite differences among tribes, Native Americans cherish some common values such as: individual freedom, respect for nature, respect for elders in the community, trust among individuals, the ability to share and care for each other's concerns, and equality for all.

 Getting Started

Ask the children to tell what they would do to find out the answer to these questions:

○ Was your state (or a neighboring state) home to a Native American nation?
○ What are the names of those tribes? Where do the descendants of those Native Americans live today?
○ Where do modern-day Native Americans live?

Have the class write a letter to your local historical society or state tourist bureau to discover answers to your questions.

▼ Reading

Book List

Nonfiction

Rediscovering Past Civilizations Series (Franklin Watts) has several different books including those on Totem Pole Indians of the Northwest, the Sioux, the Apaches, the Seminoles, and the tragedy of the Little Big Horn. There are eleven books in the series. Some of these books also appear in a paperback series titled *Full-Color First Paperbacks* (Franklin Watts).

The Sioux Indians by Sonia Bleeker (Wm. Morrow), recently reissued, is a chapter book detailing tribal life of one of the great Plains Indians nations. There are eighteen books in this popular series found in most school libraries.

In My Mother's House by Ann Nolan Clark (Viking), features Native Americans of the southwest states such as Arizona and Utah.

Explorers of the Americas Before Columbus by George DeLucenay Leon (Franklin Watts)

Indian Corn and Other Gifts by Sigmund A. Lavine (Dodd, Mead and Co.)

Native Americans–Cooperative Learning Activities by Mary Strohl and Susan Schneck (Scholastic)

Fiction

Good Hunting, Blue Sky by Peggy Parish (Harper)

Knots on a Counting Rope by Bill Martin (Henry Holt and Co.)

Sequoya by Jan Gleiter and Kathleen Thompson (Raintree Children's Books)

The Legend of Indian Paintbrush retold by Tomie dePaola (G.P. Putnam's Sons)

▼ Art

Drawing Symbols

Using what they know and can find out from the classroom library about various Native American tribes, the children can draw and color special symbols they make up for each tribal name appearing on the activity sheet on page 41. Some children may opt to use different colored squares or circles as symbols for the various tribes.

After completing the activity sheet, the children can share some of the symbols they created and talk about what gave them their ideas.

▼ Social Studies

Drawing and Using Map Keys

The children can use the symbols from the first activity sheet to draw a key and fill in the map for the activity sheet on page 42. Be aware that different books may offer conflicting information about where tribes lived and that the children should just choose one set of information for their maps. For example, the Sioux homeland was originally in areas now called southern Minnesota, Wisconsin, and northern Iowa. So some books call this area the home of the Sioux. However, around the time of the Revolutionary War, the Chippewa forced the Sioux out, and the Sioux homeland, ever since, has been mainly designated as North and South Dakota.

 Art

Making a Navaho Sand Painting

The Navaho created sand paintings to tell the tribal legends, to call forth the spirits, or to heal a sick person. To make a sand painting:

1. Soak small amounts of sand in water and different fabric dyes for a day.
2. Pour off the water and spread the sand on paper to dry.
3. Create a design on construction paper with glue. Slowly drip the colored sands on the glue and allow them to dry.

The children can display and talk about the designs.

 Crafts

Making a Tipi Model

Sioux children who lived long ago played with miniature houses just as some modern children do today. Using five drinking straws, some string, and a half-circle of paper decorated with buffalo hunting symbols, have the children make their own toy tipis. They may also use small pieces of clay at the bottom of each pole to make the tipis stand. Some children may also want to create a display of other Native American artifacts they own or can construct such as miniature snow toboggans, snowshoes, bows and arrows, dolls, or clothing.

 Writing

Making Up an Adventure Story

Following are two authentic story ideas which can serve as springboards for children's original stories:

The Windigo

Chippewas used to tell about the Windigo, a tribe of cannibals that pounced on lone hunters or gatherers in the woods. Chippewa children hearing strange noises in the night were frightened by thoughts of the dreaded, though make-believe, Windigo.

Coming of Age

In many tribes, a fifteen-year-old boy was expected to go off by himself to live in the wild and to confront hunger, animals, and bad weather with bravery. When he returned to the tribe in good health, he was considered a man, and was often given a new name signifying bravery.

 Thanksgiving Reading

Social Studies

There are many stories about the Native Americans and their relations with the Pilgrims. An especially good one is *Pocahontas and the Strangers* by Clyde Robert Bulla (Scholastic), the true story of Pocahontas, daughter of the Chief Powhatan, and her relationship with the Pilgrims of Jamestown.

The Light in the Forest by Conrad Richter (Knopf) is an exciting story and one that drives home an understanding of prejudice when children are sophisticated enough to understand it. True Son, a fifteen-year-old white boy, has lived with the Lenni Lenape since he was four. He eventually must return to his original home, but for True Son, it is a great sadness: He loves his Native American family and tribe, and he loathes life with the "weak, unhealthy" white people.

 Art

Making a Dream Catcher

Mothers of the Ojibway in Northern Minnesota had special ways of showing love for their children. One of the things a mother did was make a Dream Catcher to suspend over her sleeping child. It was thought that bad dreams come from the dark and that the Dream Catcher had powers to keep these dreams from entering a child's head. The Dream Catcher allowed the good dreams to come through.

To Make a Dream Catcher:

○ Fashion a hoop from pipe cleaners or wires.
○ Make various colored construction paper bird feathers; tie them to the hoop with yarn.
○ Beads strung on yarn or ribbons can also be tied to the hoop.

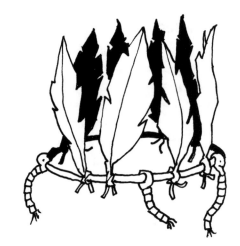

 Science

Popcorn Necklaces

Because one corn seed ultimately produces an ear with hundreds of kernels, Native Americans thought that corn contained magical qualities and believed that a powerful god placed it on earth. Native Americans discovered that corn kernels could "pop." They ate some of the popcorn, but also used it to string popcorn necklaces.

To make popcorn necklaces, pop a batch of popcorn for the class. Offer each student a thin craft needle strung with a double length of thread (approx. 24" long) knotted at the end. Have students string popcorn on the threads by passing needles carefully through popped kernels. Tie ends of thread together to create popcorn necklaces. Students may wear (and nibble on) their popcorn necklaces when taking a nature walk.

Symbols For Native American Tribes

Make up and draw a symbol for each tribe. Look in books or in the encyclopedia for ideas.

Mohawk New York	**Seminole** Florida
Sioux South Dakota	**Comanche** Texas
Navaho New Mexico	**Alabama** Texas
Mohave California	**Chinook** Washington

A Map of Native American Tribes

1. Find your state. Write its abbreviation in the correct location on the map.
2. Write the abbreviations of any other states you can locate.
3. Make a map key. Use the symbols you drew on the other activity sheet. Draw the symbols on the states to show where Native Americans lived.
4. Mount both activity sheets 1 and 2 together on a large sheet of construction paper. Symbols logged on the first sheet can be recorded in the correct locations on the map featured below. The first sheet then serves as a map key.

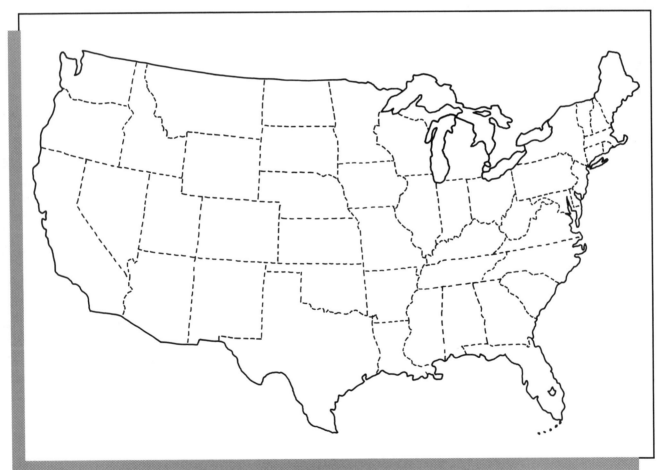

MAP KEY:

Rocks and Soil

Many children enjoy collecting rocks. Often they will pick up a rock at the park or the beach because of its interesting color, shape, texture, or sparkle. Perhaps they will be curious enough to learn the name of the rock, or something about its origin. The activities in this unit are designed to encourage children's natural interest in rocks and soil.

Getting Started

To begin the unit, show children a globe. Explain that no matter where on the earth they are standing—even if they are in a boat on the water—they are standing on or above rock.

Igneous

Then ask children to name all the things they know about rocks. List all responses—whether factually accurate or not—on the chalkboard or on chart paper. Keep the list in view as you move through the unit and allow children to add, change, or delete information as necessary. You may wish to begin each new lesson by reading the list and asking children to make revisions.

Science

Learning About the Three Types of Rocks

Metamorphic

Point out to children that each rock falls into one of three categories of rock: igneous, sedimentary, and metamorphic. Tell them that the three categories refer to the three ways rocks are formed. Create a chart like the one below on a large piece of oak tag. Help children to read the chart and encourage them to use their library research to help them add on new information.

Science

Experimenting with Rocks

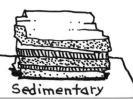

Sedimentary

You may wish to have more advanced students work in pairs or small groups to conduct their own experiments with rocks. *Science for Kids: 39 Geology Experiments* by Robert W. Wood (Tab Books) is a good source of ideas for experiments. Encourage students to share their findings with the class.

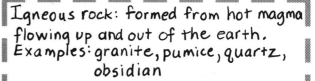

Igneous rock: formed from hot magma flowing up and out of the earth.
Examples: granite, pumice, quartz, obsidian

Sedimentary rock: formed from layers of sediment such as sand, decayed plant matter, animal bones, and shells
Examples: sandstone, shale, limestone

Metamorphic rock: formed when one kind of rock changes to another over time.
Examples: sandstone — quartzite
limestone — marble
coal — diamonds

Science

Observing Rock Changes

Rocks change over time. Their composition alters, or erosion wears them away, or they are broken into fragments by weather and plant life. To discuss the way rocks change, here are some suggestions:

○ Read a picture book such as *The Big Rock* by Bruce Hiscock (Atheneum) to children. The book details the life of a rock in the Adirondack Mountains from mountain formation through the age of the dinosaurs and to the present day.

○ Take a walk to identify instances of erosion. You might locate erosion on hills, plant-root break-up of rocks and sidewalks, and buildings worn by wind, rain, and ice.

 ## Science

Observing Sedimentary Rock Formation

Point out to children that sedimentary rocks are formed of clay, sand, gravel, and other materials that settle out of water. To illustrate the way in which sedimentary rocks are formed, try this simple demonstration. First obtain samples of sedimentary rock such as sandstone, limestone, shale, or rock salt and allow children to touch, rub, and scrape them. Can they feel the grains? Can they see layers? Then fill a glass jar with a small amount of rock fragments, sand, and some very fine sand or silt. Fill the rest of the jar with water. Cover the jar with a tight-fitting lid and shake it. Then put the jar on a flat surface and wait for the ingredients to settle. The coarser materials will go to the bottom and the lighter materials will go to the top—just as in the formation of sedimentary rock.

 ## Reading

Identifying and Naming Rocks

Accompany children to the school or local library and help them to locate books containing pictures of rocks. (Examples of suitable books are listed below.) Guide children as they compare the pictures of rocks with the rocks they collected, and help them to identify and name their rocks. Suggest that each team make a display case out of a shoebox or egg carton. Completed displays can be exhibited on shelves or tabletops.

Rock Books

Eyewitness Books: Rocks and Minerals by Dr. R. F. Symes and the staff of the Natural History Museum, London (Knopf)

The First Book of Stones by M. B. McCormick (Franklin Watts)

Rock Collecting by Roma Gans (Crowell)

Start Collecting Rocks and Minerals by Lee Ann Srogi (Running Press)

The Magic School Bus Inside the Earth by Joanna Cole (Scholastic)

Language Arts

Making Up Rock Riddles

Point out to children that people have been making things from rock since prehistoric times. Challenge children to test each other's knowledge of the practical uses of rock. Divide the class into teams of four or five players. Have each team research the practical uses of different kinds of rock to create their own rock riddles. Teams can work to answer each others' riddles, or, alternately, pool their efforts to create a Rock Riddle Book. Examples of riddles are:

1. I'm white. I'm in your house. In fact, I'm on your dinner table. You probably eat me every day. What am I? (table salt)

2. I could be in your basement. You walk on me outside your house. You play on me when you go to the playground. What am I? (the shale in cement)

3. I'm one of the hardest rocks. I'm in the walls of skyscrapers. What am I? (granite)

4. I'm considered to be very beautiful. You can wear me in jewelry. What is my name? (quartz, turquoise, or diamond)

5. I'm used to make something you can write with—something that is white and easily broken. Your teacher probably uses it all the time. What am I? (limestone in chalk)

6. I look like a sponge and am very light in weight. Although I was made of hardened lava, I keep people's heels and elbows soft. What am I? (pumice)

7. I am glassy black, brown, or green in color. Because I have a very sharp edge when I break, Native Americans used me for knives, arrowheads, and spear points. What is my name? (obsidian)

Field Notes

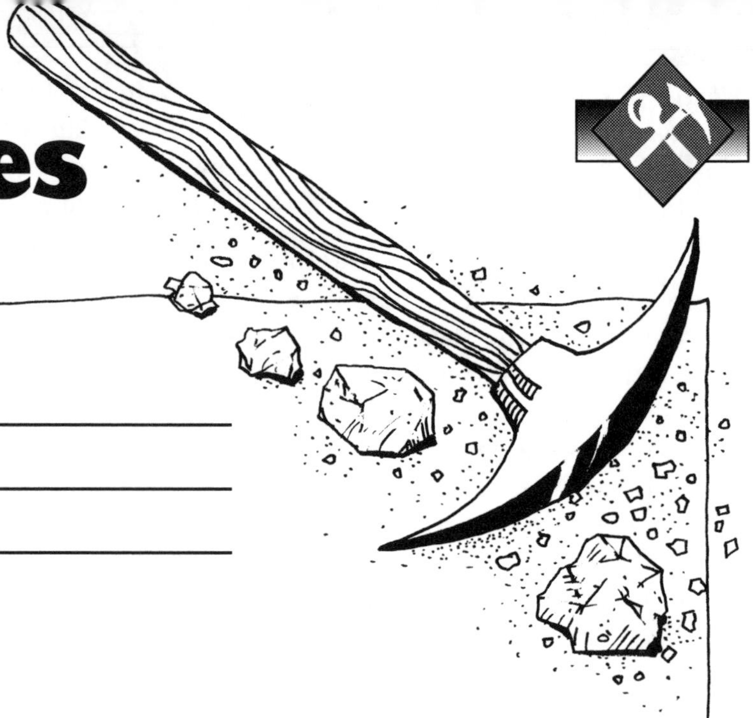

Write and Draw:

Geologist's name: _____

Date: _____

Rock site: _____

Rocks I found:

1. Which is prettiest?

_____

2. Which is most interesting?

_____

3. How do the rocks look inside?

_____

_____

Books where I found pictures of my rocks:

Book	Rock name
_____	_____
_____	_____
_____	_____
_____	_____

Skeleton Bones

In the days surrounding Halloween, skeletons are sure to come into focus. Scare up some interest in these "bags 'o bones" with the following unit.

 Fast Facts

- There are 206 bones in an adult human skeleton.
- Human bones come in many sizes and shapes: big, small, flat, round.
- Bones live and grow. A human baby has 300 bones, some of which fuse to make the final total of 206.
- Calcium makes bones hard.
- Bones hold us erect.
- Inside each bone of the skeleton is the sponge-like bone marrow. It helps to make red blood cells in the body. It also stores calcium and other nutrients we get from food.
- A sickness called rickets make bones so soft that they bend. It is caused by a lack of good nutrition.
- Joints are the places where bones meet and end. The joints in the human body enable people to move.
- The backbone has 34 bones and 33 joints that enable twisting and bending movements.
- Rib bones protect the heart and lungs. The skull bone protects the brain.
- Bones can be made stronger with good food and exercise.

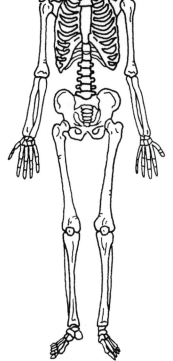

 Getting Started

To discover what the children already know about skeletons, use the list of Fast Facts to develop questions such as:

1. Why do we have bones? What would happen if you suddenly had no skeleton?
2. What do bones look like?
3. Is there anything you can do to make your skeleton grow bigger or stronger?

Using the classroom library, encourage the children to find other information about skeletons. Working in pairs, challenge each team to uncover at least one amazing skeleton fact to share with the group.

Reading

Skeleton Books:

Bones and Skeletons (Dorling Kindersley)

Eyewitness Books–Skeletons by Steve Parker (Knopf)

The Skeleton Inside You by Philip Balestrino (Scholastic)

The Skeleton and Movement by Steve Parker (Franklin Watts)

Your Wonderful Body (National Geographic Society)

The Dancing Skeleton by Cynthia DeFelice (Macmillan)

Skinny-Bones by Janet and Allan Ahlberg (William Morrow)

The Soup Bone by Tony Johnston (Harcourt Brace Jovanovich)

Have the children work in pairs with a book. Ask them to look through their books and write down a few interesting details on skeletons. Compare pairs' findings to the list of "Fast Facts."

After reading and talking about the stories, discuss reasons why skeletons are part of Halloween thrills and chills.

Movement

The Skeleton Tap Dance

Ask the children to imagine what skeletons might sound like if they were able to walk and dance. Offer the children simple percussion instruments (rhythm sticks, clickers, etc.) and ask them to keep time as you recite the following rhyme:

Take care of your skeleton
You can't live without it.
You need to care for all your bones
There's no doubt about it!

Invite children to create and act out new verses to the rhyme by offering substitutions for the word "live" (e.g. dance, stand, bend, twist, etc.).

Health

Boning Up on Bones

Have children examine a beef bone since it most closely resembles a human leg bone. Have the children look at it and comment on its appearance, texture and weight. Try comparing beef bones to chicken or turkey bones. Provide a complete set of poultry bones (which have been boiled clean) and challenge students to glue the bones back together in order to reconstruct the skeletal frame. (Check an encyclopedia for sketches of chicken skeletons.) Allow this activity to serve as a springboard to a classroom exploration of paleontology. (For more on paleontology, see "Dinosaurs" unit.)

▼ Categorizing

Bone Chart

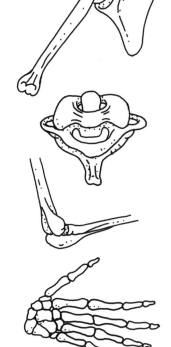

Provide students with copies of the activity sheet on page 50. Have children use the sheet to create a bone chart, categorizing bone joints according to three criteria: hinge joints, ball-in-socket joints and column joints. Begin by showing children a simple hinge, a "ball in socket" mechanism (such as pop-together plastic blocks), a long unbendable object (such as a 12″ wooden ruler) and a string of beads or plastic doughnut-shaped toys on a length of yarn. Explain that while bones themselves are unbendable (rigid) like the ruler, they may be joined or jointed together to create moveable hinges (as found at the knees and elbow joints), rotating ball-in-socket mechanisms (as found at the hip and shoulder joints) or pliable stacks of bones (as found in the spine).

Have the children palpate and move their bones in an effort to discover the rigid and the moveable parts of their skeletons.

▼ Exercise

Skeleton Dance

Prepare movement cards by labeling large index cards with the name of one bone the children have learned. Provide upbeat background music and have students take turns holding up one card. The rest of the class then refers to the cards and creates dance moves by isolating and moving only the bone (or set of bones) featured on each card.

Skeleton Bones

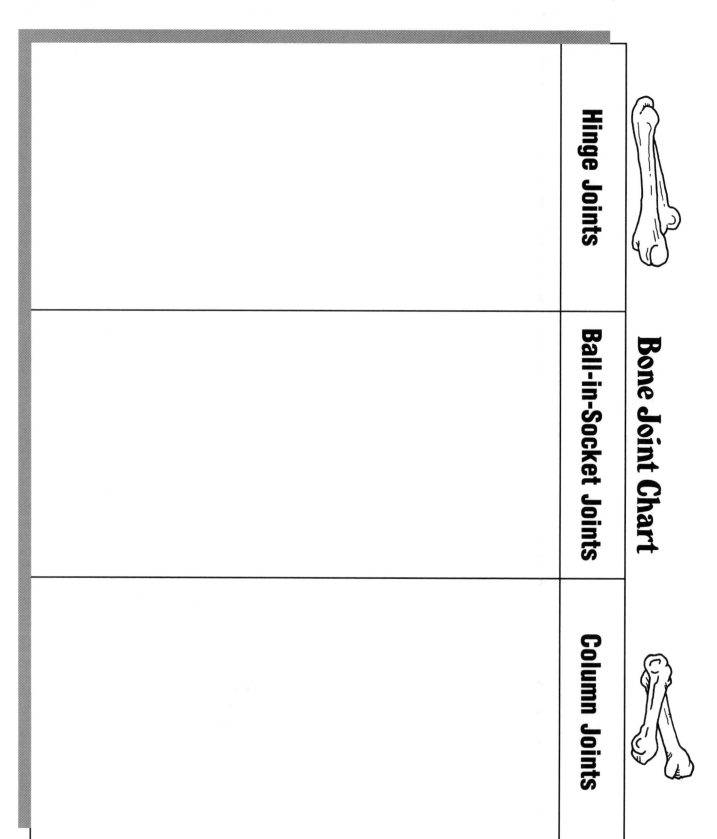

Bone Joint Chart

Hinge Joints	Ball-in-Socket Joints	Column Joints

Rhymes and Poems

Most children enjoy rhymes and rhythms, even if they have never had much formal exposure to poetry. This unit will provide lots of opportunities for your students to experience poems and rhymes through reading, writing, speaking, and art.

Getting Started

Tell students that you are going to say a word and challenge them to call out as many words as they can that rhyme with the word you call out. As the students call out their rhyme words, either you or a volunteer can write them on the chalkboard. When you feel you have enough words, end the activity by calling out "angry," "hungry," or "orange," which have few, if any, natural rhymes in English, and which will probably stump the class. Ask if any students can guess what this unit is going to be about. Most likely, the answer will be something along the lines of "poetry," or "rhymes," which is, of course, correct!

Talk with the children about the rhyming words they thought of, and why they are fun to say by themselves, in simple rhyming lines, or in poetry. If you feel it is appropriate for your students, choose one of the following rhyming verses to read to them. Then ask them to recite parts or all of any simple rhymes or poems they know.

Mix a pancake,
Stir a pancake,
Pop it in the pan;
Fry the pancake,
Toss the pancake,—
Catch it if you can.

       Christina Rossetti

Fee fi fo fum,
I smell the blood of an Englishmun.
Is he alive or is he dead?
I'll grind his bones for my bread!

       from "Jack and the Beanstalk"

I wish that my room had a floor;
I don't care so much for a door,
But this walking around
Without touching the ground
Is getting to be quite a bore.

       Gelett Burgess

There once were two cats of Kilkenny,
Each thought there was one cat too many;
So they fought and they fit,
And they scratched and they bit,
Till, excepting their nails
And the tips of their tails,
Instead of two cats, there weren't any.

Anonymous

 Reading

Enjoying Rhyming Stories

One of the best ways of enjoying rhymes is to read rhyming stories. Have the children form small groups in which to read a rhyming picture book. On subsequent days, have the groups trade books until every group has read three. Display the books on a table so that the children can enjoy them at their leisure. After most of the groups have completed the reading, have them tell which they liked best, and why. Use the activity sheet on page 55 to help students create their own rhyming stories.

Here are some suggestions for rhyming stories your students may enjoy:

Donna O'Neeshuck Was Chased by Some Cows by Bill Grossman (HarperCollins)

Crocodile Beat by Gail Jorgensen (Bradbury Press)

The Giant Jam Sandwich by John Vernon Lord and Janet Burroway (Houghton Mifflin)

hist whist by e.e. cummings (Crown)

Maxi, the Hero by Debra and Sal Barracca (Dial)

The Missing Tarts by B.G. Hennessey (Scholastic)

Possum Come a-Knockin' by Nancy Van Laan (Knopf)

Note: Many books by Dr. Seuss are written in rhyme and are widely available, easy-to-read, time-tested favorites.

 Language Arts

Listening to Poetry

Read poetry to your students, or invite interested volunteers to read to the class.

Here are some suggested anthologies and books of poetry to help you get started:

The Golden Treasury of Poetry by Louis Untermeyer (Golden Press)

Lots of Limericks selected by Myra Cohn Livingston (McElderry)

A Light in the Attic by Shel Silverstein (Harper & Row)

I Spy: A Book of Picture Riddles by Jean Marzollo (Scholastic)

A Rocket in My Pocket: The Rhymes and Chants of Young Americans by Carl Withers (Scholastic)

Rhymes and Rhythms for Laughing Out Loud; Sing a Sing of Popcorn; Every
Child's Book of Poems by Beatrice Schenk de Reginier (Scholastic Hardcover)
Poems to Tickle Your Funny Bone selected by Jack Prelutsky (Knopf)
Two-Legged, Four-Legged, No-Legged Rhymes by J. Patrick Lewis (Knopf)
Poetry Place Anthology (Scholastic)

 ## Art

Picturing Scenes in Your Mind

To help the children understand other ways to enjoy rhyming poetry, ask them to close their eyes and imagine a scene to go with this verse (or any other you choose).

The Grasshopper

The Grasshopper, the Grasshopper
I will explain to you:
He is the Brownie's race horse,
The fairy's kangaroo.

Vachel Lindsay

Read the verse a few times and point out to the children that this rhyming poem is entirely built around only two rhyming words. Then have the children draw a picture to go with the poem. While showing each other their pictures, the children can notice how many varied ideas can come from one small set of words.

 ## Social Studies

Looking at Poems from Another Culture

Help the children recall nursery rhymes from their early childhood. Then read parts of *Arroz Con Leche: Popular Songs and Rhymes from Latin America* by Lulu Delacre (Scholastic). Encourage them to take turns finding a poem they could read or memorize in English and in Spanish and then present it to the class.

Help the children find various countries in Latin America on a wall map. Have them point out any where relatives or friends were born.

 ## Music

Performing With Music

Ask the children to think of all the jump rope rhymes and silly songs they can remember as you write the titles on the chalkboard. Then have them form groups to present one of these to the class. They can change the words, sing, dance, make costumes, play rhythm band instruments or do anything to help the "audience" of other students clap wildly as they join in.

Note: Although many popular "rap" songs are inappropriate for classroom use, with a little judicious preparation on your part, you may be able to find raps that are not violent or otherwise unsuitable, and play them for your students. Children enjoy this vigorous, rhythmic musical form very much, and may wish to create their own raps after listening.

 ## Art

Making Family Gifts

The children can make placemats, one for each family member, on which they print their favorite rhyme or poem. They can draw or paint to decorate them. Encourage everyone to present the placemats at home to have some fun at meal time.

 ## Language Arts

Writing a Fold-out Rhyming Book

Remind the children of some of the rhyming stories they read in groups. Then tell them they will get a chance to write one themselves. Remind them of the pairs of rhyming words which they thought of at the beginning of the unit to help them get started.

Suggest that everyone make a first draft on plain paper. Have them read their drafts to a partner to listen for questions and suggestions.

Help the children make the fold-out book by cutting a sheet of construction paper in half, length-wise, and then pasting one end of each half to the other. They can then fold the book pages and write and draw their final version of the rhyming story. They will have to decide if they wish to have one or two or more rhyming lines per page. All volunteers should have an opportunity to read and show their finished products. Then stand the books up on a display table or shelf for a few days before they are taken home.

Name: _____

Rhyming Stories

Use the story starters below to help you create your own stories that rhyme. You can continue the story on the back of this paper.

_____ was clever, _____ was cool,

_____ was the best in the whole school.

_____

_____

_____

You'll never guess what happened to me,
It happened one day as I sat in a tree,

_____

_____

_____

Once, in a kingdom of magic,
A dragon flew in, which was tragic.

_____

_____

_____

_____

Laura Ingalls Wilder

Many children have been exposed to the stories of Laura Ingalls Wilder through the popular television series, "Little House on the Prairie." But it is the books themselves that best convey the warmth and security of family life in a world of howling wolves, raging storms, and the isolation so common to pioneer life.

 ## Getting Started

Begin the unit by reading aloud Chapter One in the first book of the series. Then lead a discussion focusing on these points and any others children may bring up:

○ Have you heard this story before? Where?
○ How does this story make you feel?
○ Would you like to have a life like Laura's? Why or why not?
○ Choose a scene from the first chapter that you liked. Are there any words or phrases that made the scene come to life?
○ Is there anything about the chapter you didn't particularly like?

Read one or more of the chapters to children each day, allowing time for discussion of unfamiliar words and concepts, new plot developments, interesting historical information, and so on.

If you choose to read aloud one chapter per day, the material in this theme unit can be covered in one week. If children read independently or in pairs, allow several weeks for completion of the unit.

 ## Reading

Finding Out About the Author

Point out that authors often use their own lives to provide inspiration for their works of fiction. Encourage children to read biographies or autobiographies about the life of Wilder. Then have them share their ideas about how Wilder's life was reflected in the books she wrote.

The First Four Years by Laura Ingalls Wilder (Scholastic)

Laura Ingalls Wilder by Gwen Blair (Putnam)

Laura Ingalls Wilder: Growing Up in the Little House by Patricia Reilly Giff (Viking)

On the Way Home: The Diary of a Trip from South Dakota to Mansfield, Missouri, in 1884 by Laura Ingalls Wilder (HarperCollins)

These Happy Golden Years by Laura Ingalls Wilder (Scholastic)

West From Home: Letters of Laura Ingalls Wilder edited by Roger Lea MacBride (Harper & Row)

✓ Reading and Social Studies

The Ingalls Family Saga

You may want to have your class continue reading other books about the Ingalls family. Whether you read the books aloud or have children read them independently, track the Ingalls's movement on a wall map of the United States as the family moves from place to place. The following is a complete list of the books in the series.

Little House in the Big Woods, Wisconsin. This book begins the series in the 1870s where we meet Laura, her two sisters, and her father and mother. We observe them in the warmth and safety of their lamp-lit home while outside, in the wilderness, wolves and bears and the raging storms pose a constant threat.

Little House on the Prairie, Wisconsin, Minnesota, Iowa, Missouri, Oklahoma. The cozy safety of family life sustains Laura through catastrophes such as a devastating prairie fire and an onslaught by a pack of wolves.

On the Banks of Plum Creek, Minnesota. Within a few miles of their home there are other families and Laura has the chance to go to school and make friends.

By the Shores of Silver Lake, North Dakota. The family now moves between their home on the lake and one they have built in a small town.

The Long Winter, North Dakota. Though the family now lives in town, the challenges they face (such as a life-threatening blizzard) and the strength it takes to meet them makes this book one of the most exciting in the series.

Little Town on the Prairie tells about Laura as she grows up, becomes a teacher, and marries Almanzo Wilder—whose family's story is told in *Farmer Boy.*

✓ Creative Dramatics

Acting Out the Story

Children will enjoy planning, rehearsing, and performing a play based on their reading of *Little House in the Big Woods.*

Have children working in small groups choose a dramatic scene from the book that they would like to perform. Suggest that children read the scene again and make a list of the characters involved. Have each group assign roles, keeping in mind the fact that a theatrical production involves important nonacting jobs, too—for instance, a director, a prop person, and a costume person. Encourage children to make sure that everyone in the group has a job, and that the job is suited to their interests and abilities.

Plays—whether scripted or nonscripted—should arise out of a series of group improvisations. Dialogue, bits of stage business, and other elements that seem to work best are noted and saved for the final production.

Allow time for all groups to present their scenes. After each presentation, be sure to provide an opportunity for others in the class to ask questions and offer comments. You may want to combine the efforts of all the groups and present the plays as a series. Other classes or parents could be invited to the performance.

 Language Arts

Listening to Stories at Home

Ask children to think about the stories Pa told his children—stories from his own life and boyhood. Do their family members ever tell them stories about the past? Guide children to see that some of the best stories we hear are stories that come from our own families. Encourage children to ask parents, grandparents, and other relatives to tell them stories about their childhoods. Allow time for students to share these stories with the class.

After children share their stories, you may wish to invite some of the original storytellers—the parents, grandparents, or other relatives—to class to recount incidents from their lives. Try tape-recording their stories. Later, play the recordings for children and discuss what the storytellers did to make their stories particularly interesting.

For more information on storytelling, you may wish to consult *Storytelling: A Guide for Teachers* by Catherine Farrell (Scholastic).

 Language Arts and Art

Using a Picture for Storytelling

Invite children to imagine that they are city cousins of Laura who visit her for the first time in the little house in the big woods. How does Laura's life compare with their own? What are their impressions of the way Laura lives? Then ask children to think of an exciting adventure that happens during the visit. Have children brainstorm possible ideas for adventures, and write their suggestions on the chalkboard.

Then distribute copies of the activity sheet on page 60. Tell children that they are going to draw a picture of their adventure. Have them draw in background details such as the barn and the corral with livestock. The invite children to draw their adventure, placing themselves in the picture along with Laura and her family. After the pictures are completed, encourage children to tell their adventure stories to the class using their pictures as a graphic aid. Before they tell their stories, discuss with children what makes a good storyteller. Suggest certain techniques such as:

○ planning what to say,
○ speaking loudly and clearly,
○ making eye contact with the audience, and
○ using both the voice and face to create suspense.

Art

Making Pioneer Dolls

Remind children that Laura's first doll was made from a corn cob. Would children of today be happy with a doll like that? Is it necessary to buy a manufactured doll whose hair grows and turns colors when you dip her in water? Challenge children to use their ingenuity to make dolls out of materials they might find at home. Have children work in pairs to come up with imaginative ideas and solutions such as:

○ puppets made from socks
○ rag dolls made from bits of cloth and yarn
○ beanbag dolls
○ paper dolls
○ marionettes made from ice-cream sticks.

After the dolls are completed, encourage children to show their work to the class and discuss how the dolls were made.

 Social Studies

Other Times, Other Cultures

Laura Ingalls Wilder wrote about a particular time and a particular group of people who held certain beliefs. Some of these beliefs are considered objectionable by today's standards. Ask children if they can think of instances in the book in which unfair ideas or opinions are expressed by the characters—or by the writer. Children may mention the father's treatment of his children, the role of women, and negative references to Native Americans and African Americans. Why do they think pioneer families such as the Ingalls were often so intolerant of differences? Are people today more tolerant? Does the fact that some of the characters hold unacceptable beliefs make the book less enjoyable to read?

Encourage children to ask their parents, grandparents, or older relatives about how children were brought up when they were small. How were children disciplined? How much independence did they get? If children and parents disagreed, how were their differences settled? Ask children to jot down notes and report their findings to the class.

 Science

Making Home-Made Bookmarks

Children will enjoy making home-made bookmarks they can use with the Wilder books and others. Remind children that when the weather was warm, the Ingalls children spent much of their time outside playing in the grass. Take children on a field trip. Have them collect interesting grasses, leaves, weeds, and wildflowers. Back in the classroom, suggest that children choose two or three specimens they like and press them between waxed paper in a heavy book for one week. Then give them long strips of oaktag on which to arrange and paste the specimens. Some children may want to paint or draw designs on the bookmarks as well. When the bookmarks are dry, help children to cover them in see-through plastic wrap. They can use their bookmarks in school, at home, or give them as gifts.

Name: _____

Laura Ingalls Wilder

Make up a story and put yourself in it. Draw the details in the picture. Add you, Laura, the barn, wolves, bears, storms, or anything to make a good picture adventure.

Fear in the Big Woods

_____
_____
_____
_____
_____
_____
_____
_____
_____

WINTER

December Celebrations

The holidays Christmas, Hanukkah, and Kwanzaa share certain similarities. Children may mention the fact that all these holidays are celebrated in the month of December, or that several of the holidays involve getting together with families, and gift-giving rituals. There are other similarities, too, and they will learn about them in this unit.

 ## Getting Started

Ask children if they can identify some of the things these holidays have in common.

Prepare a bulletin board display like the one below, making sure to leave space in the center of the display. As they go through the unit, children can fill in characteristics common to the holidays.

 ## Reading

December Celebrations

As holiday time approaches, encourage children to go to the library to find these and other books about holiday celebrations. You may wish to set aside a special shelf in your classroom in which books are arranged according to holiday. Encourage children to peruse these books at their leisure.

The Birds' Christmas Carol by Kate Douglas Wiggin (Scholastic)

The Chanukah Guest by Eric Kimmel (Scholastic)

The Christmas Coat by Clyde Robert Bulla (Knopf)

The Christmas Sky by Franklyn Branley (HarperCollins)

A Christmas Memory by Truman Capote (Knopf)

The Christmas Secret by Joan Lexau (Scholastic)

Hanukah Money by Sholem Aleichem (Mulberry)

Have a Happy . . . by Mildred Pitts Walter (Lothrop, Lee)

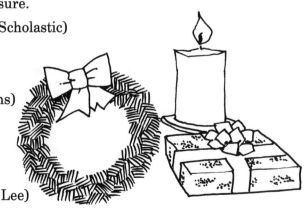

It's Christmas by Jack Prelutsky (Scholastic)

Kwanzaa by Deborah Newton Chocolate (Children's Press)

Kwanzaa by A. P. Porter (Carolrhoda)

Las Navidades by Lulu Delacre (Scholastic)

Latkes and Applesauce by Fran Manushkin (Scholastic)

A Picture Book of Hanukkah by David Adler (Scholastic)

 ## Social Studies

Learning About Kwanzaa

Ask children if any of them celebrate Kwanzaa. Do they know what Kwanzaa is all about? Fill in the gaps in children's knowledge with these facts:

○ Kwanzaa is a nonreligious African-American celebration that was invented in the 1970's.
○ It is based on various African harvest celebrations.
○ Kwanzaa begins on December 26 and continues for 7 days.

During each of the days of Kwanzaa, family members gather to light one of seven candles. As each candle burns, the family discusses one of the seven principles on which Kwanzaa is based:

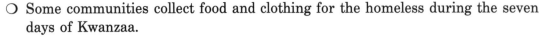

1. Unity
2. Self-determination
3. Collective responsibility
4. Cooperative economics
5. Purpose
6. Creativity
7. Faith

○ Some communities collect food and clothing for the homeless during the seven days of Kwanzaa.
○ On the seventh night, there is a feast to which friends and extended family members are invited. There are traditional foods, and cards and gifts are exchanged (although the giving of expensive commercial items is de-emphasized in favor of simple, handmade gifts). There is also singing and dancing.
○ People greet each other with the Swahili expression *"Habari gani,"* which means "What's new?" This is followed by a response that relates to one of the seven principles.

 ## Social Studies

Discussing the Principles of Kwanzaa

Divide the class into seven groups and assign each group one of the seven principles of Kwanzaa. Tell children that their job is to explain the meaning of one of the principles to the class. Before children meet in their groups, discuss ways that the groups can go about their research. Suggestions include looking up unfamiliar words in a dictionary, looking up Kwanzaa in the encyclopedia or another reference work, talking to someone who might celebrate Kwanzaa, and discussing possible meanings within the group.

When the groups are ready, each group can present its explanation to the class.

☑ Social Studies

Finding Out About Hanukkah

Ask children who celebrate Hanukkah to tell how their families celebrate the holiday. Then broaden the discussion to include the rest of the class; ask children to name one fact they know about Hanukkah. List their comments on the chalkboard and supplement their knowledge with the following facts:

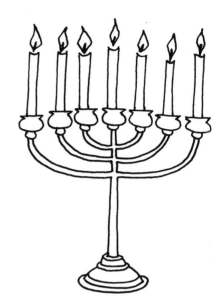

○ Hanukkah, or the "Festival of Light," is celebrated by Jews all over the world.

○ Hanukkah celebrates the taking back of the Temple of Jerusalem from the Romans over two thousand years ago.

○ When the Temple was destroyed, the lamp of the Eternal Light, which symbolized the continuation of the Jewish people, was snuffed out. Only enough oil to light the lamp for one day was found. But because of a "miracle," the lamp burned for eight days— enough time for the temple to be rededicated.

○ Hanukkah is celebrated with a menorah—a lamp holding eight candles—to symbolize this miracle. On each of the eight days of Hanukkah, a candle is lit.

○ There is no special feast, but traditional foods—especially *latkes*—are served. *Latkes* are fried potato pancakes. Friends and extended family are usually invited to the celebration, which usually includes the singing of Hanukkah songs.

○ Children sometimes exchange gifts and often receive "Hanukkah gelt," or coins. They also play a game with a "dreidl," or a spinning top with four flat sides.

☑ Social Studies

Comparing Holidays

Go back to the bulletin board and have children suggest other ways holidays they discussed are similar. Add these ideas to the display. Then ask why they think people everywhere—including those who lived long ago—enjoy celebrating these holidays.

Distribute copies of the activity sheet on page 67 and go over it with children. Encourage children to work independently. After children have completed their sheets, ask them to share their work with a partner. Do their partners know the answers to their questions? Can they suggest books that might contain such information?

Art

Making a Dreidl

Have children ask family members to help them cut down a milk carton so that only the bottom two inches remain. Family members can also make a tiny hole in the center of the bottom of the carton through which a pencil can be poked.

Have children glue strips of blue paper to the sides of the carton and label each side with a letter: **N** (for nothing), **G** (for all), **H** (for half), and **S** (for put). Help children to poke a pencil through the hole in the carton and allow them to practice spinning their dreidls.

Encourage pairs of children to play the game of "dreidl." Each pair starts out with a pot of "goodies" (use nuts, raisins, beads, or checkers in lieu of candy or pennies). Depending upon how the dreidl lands, participants take nothing, all, or half the pot—or put back everything they have already won.

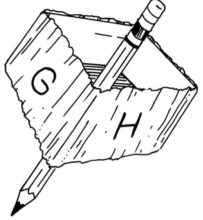

 Art and Language Arts

Drawing and Talking About Christmas Scenes

Since Christmas has such high visibility in the United States, all children in your class are likely to know something of its origins and practices: most likely, many of them celebrate it. Encourage children to make drawings depicting what it is they most enjoy about Christmas or the Christmas season.

As children present as discuss their pictures, list images of the holiday on the chalkboard as they appear in children's drawings. Examples are gifts, trees, yule logs, candles, lights, church, Santa Claus.

After all children have shared their pictures, go over the list with children and have them add any other images they can think of that can be identified with Christmas.

December Holidays

Draw a picture for each holiday in the space provided. What else would you like to know about each one? Write a question about it on the lines. How can you find out the answers?

KWANZAA

Question: _____

HANUKKAH

Question: _____

CHRISTMAS

Question: _____

Martin Luther King, Jr.

Dr. Martin Luther King, Jr. is one of the twentieth century's most influential Americans. His commitment to non-violence never wavered, even in the face of outrageous provocation. That commitment gave him great legitimacy and power. He will always be a role model for all people to follow in times of conflict or change.

⚡ Fast Facts

❍ Martin Luther King, Jr. was born the second of three children in Atlanta, Georgia, January 15, 1929.

❍ King's father and his maternal grandfather were ministers with strong public speaking capabilities.

❍ King's childhood was happy, though his parents had to explain the meaning of "prejudice" and "segregation" to King when he was a small boy.

❍ King skipped the ninth and twelfth grades and then attended Morehouse College, where he was found to be behind his classmates, because his previous school had not adequately prepared him for college. However, he worked hard, and soon made good grades.

❍ King attended Crozer Theological Seminary where he learned of the peaceful and victorious movement developed by Mahatma Ghandi that gained India's freedom from England in 1947.

❍ King earned a doctorate from Boston University and later married Coretta Scott.

❍ Dr. King became the pastor at the Dexter Avenue Baptist Church in Montgomery, Alabama.

❍ In December of 1953 in Montgomery, a black woman named Mrs. Rosa Parks refused to give up her seat on a bus when asked to by a white man. Dr. King was called to lead a movement changing the Alabama laws about bus segregation.

❍ To fight against the unfair treatment on the buses, King began to preach the practice of nonviolence and "passive resistance." Eleven months of protests and praying over the Rosa Parks incident paid off. The government revoked the existing law and bus seating was desegregated.

❍ For the next ten years, King organized demonstrations, gave speeches, and marched to get the Civil Rights Bill passed in Congress. This bill outlawed school segregation and allowed all adults with a sixth grade education to vote.

○ In 1963, the largest demonstration for civil rights ever held was lead by Dr. King. The crowd, including people of all ethnic backgrounds, numbered 250,000.

○ King and other civil rights workers planned a fifty-four mile march from Selma, Alabama to Montgomery, Alabama. The marchers were stopped on two separate occasions by Alabama police, but the world press protested and the third march finished peacefully. This march resulted in having the Voting Rights Act being signed into law.

○ In 1964, Dr. King won the Nobel Prize for peace. At 34 years of age, he was the youngest person ever to receive the prize.

○ In April 1968, at the age of thirty-nine, Dr. Martin Luther King, Jr. was assassinated.

Getting Started

Ask the children to tell what they know about Dr. Martin Luther King, Jr. Share a read-aloud biography or two from the list of suggested books (below). Ask children to talk about what kind of man they think Dr. King probably was. Make a list of attributes the children associate with Dr. King. Have them speculate as to why some people disliked or hated Dr. King and why anyone would want to end his life.

Reading

Book List

A Picture Book of Martin Luther King by David Adler (Scholastic)

Martin Luther King, Jr. A Picture Story by Margaret Boone-Jones (Children's Press)

You Can Make a Difference by Anne Bailey (Bantam Skylark)

Martin Luther King, Jr. by Diane Patrick (Franklin Watts)

Rosa Parks: My Story by Rosa Parks and Jim Haskins (Dial)

Language Arts

Divide the class into small groups. Assign each group a term from the following list:

freedom	prejudice
civil rights	segregation
equality	peace
nonviolent	dream

Have groups use dictionaries to define each word in general and then use biographies to define each word as it relates specifically to the life and work of Martin Luther King, Jr. Have each group record their findings on a piece of oaktag by writing the general definition at the top of the paper, and a sentence including the word as it relates to Dr. King at the bottom of the paper. Children can then use the space in-between to illustrate their sentences about Dr. King.

Critical Thinking Skills

Exploring Reactions to Unfair Situations

Not all children know what it feels like to be ostracized or prejudged because of their skin color, but most children know what it feels like to be in situations that seem unfair or unjust.

After having children describe such unfair times they've experienced, have the class brainstorm possible reactions to the problems. Try to be accepting of any and all reactions—even those you feel may be undesirable or ineffective (such as "hitting" or "being unfair back"). Divide a large piece of paper into three equal columns. In the first column, record the children's dilemmas. In the middle column, record possible reactions to each dilemma.

Down the right hand side of the paper, record some possible consequences to each reaction. Have the group debate which reaction(s) would most likely result in the best solutions.

For a follow-up activity, make copies of the cards on page 72 which feature unfair dilemmas common to childhood. Cut the cards apart and place in a box or bag. Students may take turns pulling a card, reading it to the group, and talking about positive ways to cope with each situation.

Variation:

Use a marker to divide each sheet of a supply of drawing paper in half horizontally. On the top half of each sheet of drawing paper, glue a dilemma card. Children should use the top half of the page to illustrate the dilemma, and the bottom half of the page to illustrate and write about a possible positive solution. If desired, papers may be displayed individually or bound together into a book titled, "Problem Solving Ideas."

 Language Arts

Writing a Story of Courage

When he stood up for what he believed in without hurting other people in the process, Martin Luther King, Jr. demonstrated that he was a man of great courage. Help children to understand that, in some ways, it might have been easier for Dr. King and his followers to use physical power to fight back against injustice rather than relying on nonviolent solutions to an angry situation. Invite children to talk about times they have been courageous and have them think of other courageous people they know and admire. Remind children that people can be courageous in small and quiet ways. Supply each student with a copy of the activity sheet on page 71 which helps them recount a time they were courageous.

Courage

BADGE OF COURAGE

1. How can you explain the word courage?

   _____
   _____
   _____

2. Tell about a time that you were afraid but tried to be courageous:

   _____
   _____
   _____

3. How does it feel to be courageous?

   _____
   _____
   _____

4. List the names of some people you know who must be courageous every day. Next to each name, give the reason he or she must be brave:

   _____
   _____
   _____

Dr. Martin Luther King, Jr.

Unfair Dilemma Cards

Cut on the dotted lines. Place the cards in a box or bag and, with your classmates, take turns selecting a card and telling how you would deal with the situation it describes.

You've waited patiently for a turn on the playground swing. Just as your turn begins, the bell rings and recess is over.

Your parents won't let you have a dog, even though you promise to take care of it.

Your mother won't give you money for candy, even though all your friends' mothers give them candy money.

You know an answer to a difficult question, but the teacher doesn't call on you.

Your friends make fun of you because you don't own the best brand of sneakers.

Your bedtime is one hour earlier than your friend's bedtime.

Your brother or sister breaks a vase and blames you.

You did your homework but lost it on the way to school. Your teacher says you'll have to do it again.

When team captains choose players, you're always chosen last.

Weather

Everybody may talk about the weather, but you and your students can do something about it. Students will enjoy reading weather poems, making a rain gauge, and learning weather folklore in this unit about weather.

 ## Fast Facts

- ❍ The earth is surrounded by a blanket of gases called the atmosphere, which extends about six hundred miles above the earth's surface.
- ❍ The atmosphere protects the earth from the sun's rays. The upper atmosphere is quite still: It is in the six miles closest to the earth that weather occurs, with all its motion and turbulence.
- ❍ The sun is the most important element in our weather, causing wind, rain, snow, fog, thunder, hail (and, of course, sunshine).
- ❍ Air masses greatly affect weather. Cold air masses are heavy, and produce low pressure. Warm air rises, producing high pressure. The invisible boundary between two air masses is called a front. Clouds are probably the most easily-observed weather characteristic. There are several types, including:
  Cumulus–small, airy clouds that appear on sunny days.
  Cumulonimbus–large, dark thunder clouds.
  Cirrus–feathery, slender bands or patches of thin, white, fleecy clouds.
  Cirrocumulus–a series of small, regularly-shaped clouds that look like ripples or grains.
- ❍ Meteorology is the science dealing with atmospheric phenomena, particularly weather.

 ## Getting Started

Ask the children to describe all of the different types of weather that usually occur in your area. As they call out the weather condition, write the word on the board, as a column heading. After the types of weather have been listed, ask children to name the kinds of activities they enjoy during each different type of weather. Write the activities under the column headings on the board. On an unused section of the chalkboard where it

Sun	Rain	Snow
go to the park	look for worms	make a snowman
play with my dog	play inside	slide down the hill
ride my bike	paint a picture	ski
go to the beach	listen to the sound of the rain	make a snow castle
play ball	brush my dog	make lots of foot prints
fly my kite	try on my ear-rings	shovel our front walk

is likely to be undisturbed for the duration of the unit, make a list of all the questions students have about weather. Encourage them to add more questions as they think of them on subsequent days. Invite students to cross out questions as they are answered, and add new questions as they occur.

Reading

Weather Books

Help the children collect weather books such as these to set up a classroom library:

Eyewitness Books Weather by Bryan Cosgrove (Knopf)

Flash, Crash, Rumble, and Roll by Franklyn Branley (Crowell)

Lightning and Thunder by Herbert S. Zim (Morrow)

The Science Book of Air by Neil Ardley (Harcourt Brace Jovanovich)

Snow and Ice by Stephen Krensky (Scholastic)

The Snowy Day by Ezra Jack Keats (Scholastic)

Weather and Climate by George and Anne Purvis (Bookwright Press)

What Will the Weather Be? by Lynda DeWitt (HarperCollins)

What Will the Weather Be Like Today? by Paul Rogers (Scholastic)

White Snow, Bright Snow by Alvin Tresselt (Scholastic)

Tornado Alert by Franklyn Branley (HarperCollins)

Have volunteers choose one question from the list, and use the classroom library to answer it. Invite students to report their findings. Encourage listeners to ask questions and add any information on the subject that *they* have also found.

Science

Recording Data and Making Predictions

Do this activity close to dismissal time. Take your class outdoors and have them observe the weather, paying particular attention to the clouds. Provide them with notebooks in which to record the date, the temperature ("hot," "warm," or "cold," will do), and a sketch of any clouds they observe. Ask them to predict what kind of weather they will have tomorrow, based on their observations. Ask them to take their notebooks home and review their observations as they watch the TV news weather report. When they return to school the next day, invite them to discuss their predictions, and how they compared with the newscasters'. Did any of them predict the weather accurately? If so, discuss the factors that might have contributed to that accuracy. Help the students draw inferences. Continue the activity for several days, during which time students' predictions should become more accurate as they begin to notice correlations between the cloud conditions and temperatures on the afternoon of one day and the weather of the next. Although the children will not become expert weather forecasters, this activity will exercise their observation and thinking skills.

Science and the Environment

Classroom Clouds

You don't have to leave the classroom to watch a cloud form. The following activity will help students understand how clouds are made.

Materials:

a 2 qt. (or 2 L) glass bottle with a narrow neck (empty apple and cranberry juice bottles are good)
hot, soapy water
a match

1. Wash the mouth of the bottle with the soapy water. Dry the mouth off, then hold the bottle upside down.
2. Either you or another adult hold a lit match inside the mouth of the bottle for about five seconds. **(Caution: Be sure only adults handle matches.)**
3. Remove the match and wait a minute or two to let the bottle cool. Then invite a student volunteer to cover the bottle opening with her or his mouth, and try to blow air into the bottle.
4. Have the volunteer take his or her mouth away from the bottle. Ask: What's happening inside the bottle? How do you think the cloud formed? Encourage discussion.

 ## Language Arts

Reading and Listening to Beautiful Words

You can find weather poems in almost all anthologies for children. Volunteers can find and read good ones to the class. Good books for this purpose are:

A January Fog Will Freeze a Hog and Other Weather Folklore by Hubert Davis (Crown), and *Poetry Place Anthology* (Scholastic).

Math

Making a Rain Gauge

Have the children research rain gauges by looking in the tables of contents or indexes of the classroom library books. Help them recall that TV weather forecasters usually talk about how many inches of rain fall. Have the children work in pairs or groups to obtain cans and jars to measure the rainfall in the school yard.

Discuss the activity sheet on page 77, and then have the children use it to carry out the experiment.

The children will note that different groups record different results. Ask them to speculate on the reasons for this. (The circumference of the container is one reason, the variation in rainfall is another.)

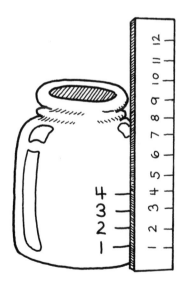

▼ Language Arts

Listening to and Illustrating Poetry

Read or copy one or more of the following poems and have the children choose crayons, chalk, watercolor or tempera to illustrate one they like.

One Misty, Moisty Morning
Anonymous

One misty, moisty morning,
 When cloudy was the weather,
I chanced to meet an old man,
 Clothed all in leather.
He began to compliment
 And I began to grin.
How do you do? And how do you do?
 And how do you do again?

First Snow
by Marie Louise Allen

Snow makes whiteness where it falls.
The bushes look like popcorn-balls.
And places where I always play,
Look like somewhere else today.

Rhyme
by Elizabeth Coatsworth

I like to see a thunder storm,
 a dunder storm,
 A blunder storm,
I like to see it, black and slow,
Come tumbling down the hills.

I liked to hear a thunder storm,
 a plunder storm,
 A wonder storm,
Roar loudly at our little house
And shake the window sills!

August Heat
Anonymous

In August, when the days are hot,
I like to find a shady spot,
And hardly move a single bit-
And sit-
 And sit-
 And sit-
 And sit!

I'm Glad the Sky Is Painted Blue
Anonymous

I'm glad the sky is painted blue,
 And the earth is painted green,
With such a lot of nice fresh air
 All sandwiched in between.

Making A Rain Gauge

A rain gauge measures the amount of rain that falls in a certain area. To make a rain gauge, you will need:
- ○ a see-through glass or plastic jar with a wide mouth
- ○ a ruler
- ○ a waterproof marker

Setting up the experiment:

1. Use a ruler to mark the side of the jar. Put a mark one inch from the bottom, another at two inches, another at three inches, and so on, up to the top of the jar.
2. Place the jar outdoors in an area where it will be able to catch rain, but where it will be safe from being knocked over.

Observing the experiment:

1. Wait for rain. Notice the time when the rain starts and write it down: _____
2. When it stops, check the amount of rain in the jar. Notice the time when the rain stops, and write it down: _____
3. Write down the number of inches of rain: _____
4. Subtract the time when the rain started from the time when the rain stopped to find out how long it rained.
5. It rained _____ inches in _____ (minutes or hours.)

Compare your results with the others in your class. Is there a difference? Why do you think there is a difference?

_____

_____

_____

_____

_____

Giants: A Unit About Self-Esteem

A child's self-esteem is not inborn; instead, it develops and evolves in response to the child's experiences and environment. In this unit, children learn techniques and strategies that will help to improve their feelings of self-worth and guide them to acknowledge the worth of others.

▶ Getting Started

To start the unit, discuss with children the concept of "giant" as evidenced in the following expressions: "giant in the sports world," "giant in the science world," "giant among people." What makes someone a giant? Guide children to think of people—famous or not-so-famous—who are "giants."

Ask children to think of words to describe these giants, such as: *powerful, gentle, helpful, smart.* Then write the word *self-esteem* on the chalkboard. Do children know what it means? Tell children that self-esteem means feeling good about yourself. Then ask children to imagine a giant of self-esteem. What words might describe such a giant? As children dictate the words, write them on separate strips of paper and save them to use in the next activity.

☑ Art

Making a Self-Esteem Bulletin Board

To make a Self-Esteem Bulletin Board, outline a giant's arms, legs, and head on large pieces of oak tag and cut out the pieces. Have children color them and draw in features. Mount the pieces on a bulletin board, leaving an empty area for the giant's torso. Then have children place the word strips from the above activity in the empty area on the giant to make the giant's torso. Children can make the giant grow by adding other word strips as they go through the unit activities.

☑ Language Arts

Writing a Feeling Diary

Locate a copy of *Feelings* by Aliki (Mulberry). Ask a volunteer to read a page a day, until the book is finished. Use the pictures on the page to talk about feelings. What are they? Does everybody have them? Ask children to name all the kinds of feelings they can think of and list their suggestions on the chalkboard. Guide children to see that we are very much alike when it comes to our emotions.

Ask children to write a diary of their feelings every day for five days. Suggest that they write three feelings they had that day, and to jot down an event, memory, thought, conversation, or experience that caused them to experience that feeling.

☑ Critical Thinking

Thinking About Making Mistakes

Write the following sentence on the chalkboard and ask children what they think it means:

People who never make mistakes are people who don't do anything.

Then read aloud the following poem:

Mistake, mistake
I made a mistake.
I baked the garbage
and threw out the cake.

Wrong, wrong,
This time I'm wrong.
But being wrong
Is not so life-long.

Lead children in a discussion about mistakes and their impact on self-esteem. Guide children to see that making honest mistakes helps us to learn and grow. Encourage children to share with the class mistakes they have made. How did they feel after making the mistake? How did others respond to their mistake? Did they feel they learned something from having made the mistake?

☑ Language Arts

Writing and Personal Best

Encourage children to write a book in two chapters entitled "The Best About Me." The first chapter can describe a character who has low self-esteem; the second, how that character's self-esteem is increased as he or she grows and changes. Before writing, ask children to brainstorm ideas about different kinds of things that could increase one's self-esteem. When the books are finished, ask children to illustrate them and share them with the class. You might wish to set up a table in the classroom where the books can be displayed. Encourage children to peruse each others' work at their leisure.

☑ Language Arts

Listening to Stories

Read a giant story to children and allow them time to respond. To start the discussion, you might ask questions such as: What is the giant in the story like? Is this giant like the ones they discussed? Why or why not? Why do they think giants in literature are so often depicted as scary? The following is a list of giant books you might like to read aloud to children.

Giant Books

Fin M'Coul: The Giant of Knockmany Hill by Tomie de Paola (Holiday House)

Giant John by Arnold Lobel (Harper & Row)

The Giant's Farm by Jane Yolen (Harcourt Brace Javonovich)

The Good Giants and the Bad Pukwudgies by Jean Fritz (Putnam's)

Jack and the Beanstalk by Beatrice Schenk De Regniers (McElderry)

Molly Whuppie by Walter de la Mar (Farrar, Strauss & Giroux)

The Selfish Giant by Oscar Wilde (Scholastic)

 Creative Dramatics

Putting On a Play About Self-Esteem

Discuss with children the fact that everyone experiences hurt feelings now and then, but that it is important not to let those feelings affect one's basic feeling of self-worth. Encourage children to brainstorm scenarios in which an individual's self-esteem is threatened. Write children's ideas on the chalkboard. Possible scenarios include:

○ I'm chosen last for a team.
○ Everyone can hit a baseball but me.
○ My best friend has a new best friend.
○ Someone I like says something about me behind my back.
○ I've hurt someone's feelings and I feel awful.
○ My clothes aren't as nice as other kids' clothes.

Have children working in small groups to create short plays exploring a situation in which a character experiences feelings of low self-esteem. After each group has presented their play, ask other children to respond to what they saw. Guide children's responses with questions such as: Did this ever happen to you or to someone you know? What can you do so a situation like this won't affect your self-esteem? What can tell yourself? What can you tell others?

 Social Studies

Helping Others To Increase Their Self-Esteem

Have children work with a partner. Ask children to tell their partners about something they would like to try but think they can't do; for instance, riding a skateboard, hitting a baseball, keeping their room organized, being more tolerant of a younger sibling. Allow time for the partners to meet each day for a week and keep notes on each others' progress in this area, giving support and encouragement as needed. At the end of a week, allow children to "brag" to the class about the accomplishments of their partners.

Social Studies and Art

Making a Coat-of-Arms

In the middle ages, special crests designed with mottos, emblems, or other symbols were worn by nobility as a sign of pride in themselves and their families. Suggest that children create personal coats-of-arms. Give each child a copy of the activity sheet on page 82. The children can then use the sheet to create their own coats-of-arms.

Children can use their imaginations to create symbols and mottos, words and phrases, or a combination of each, to answer the following questions. The number of each segment on the coat-of-arms corresponds to the number of the question.

1. What do I do that makes me feel most proud of myself?
2. What is the best thing about my family?
3. If I had guaranteed success, what thing would I most want to do?
4. What three things would I most like people to say about me?

Children may wish to seal their coats-of-arms with clear self-stick paper and attach them to their clothing with safety pins. Allow time for children to admire each other's work.

 Emotional Health

Learning to Love Yourself

Do you have to be born a giant, or can you become one? Can children think of individuals—historical figures, characters from literature or the movies, or perhaps people they know—whose self-esteem increased as they grew up and learned to love themselves? The following books focus on characters who succeed in life when they learn to accept themselves for who they are.

Leo, the Late Bloomer by Robert Kraus (Windmill)

Crow Boy by Taro Yashima (Viking)

The Beast in Mrs. Rooney's Room by Patricia Reilly Giff (Dell)

Ramona Quimby, Age Eight by Beverly Cleary (Morrow)

Call it Courage by Armstrong Sperry (Scholastic)

Choose these and other books about self-esteem and set aside time every day for children to read in pairs. After children have finished their books, encourage them to discuss what they have read. Raise such questions as: How did the character feel about him/herself at the beginning of the book? At the end of the book? What happened along the way to cause the character to experience a change in self-esteem? Is there something that happened to you that caused you to feel good about yourself? What was it?

Name: _____

My Coat of Arms

Answer the questions below, and then make up a symbol to represent your answer. (For example, if the best thing about your family is your father's great spaghetti sauce, the symbol for that might be a big, steaming bowl of spaghetti.) Draw your symbol in the space on the coat-of-arms that has the same number as the question that the symbol answers. Display your finished coat-of-arms with pride!

1. What do I do that makes me feel most proud of myself?
2. What is the best thing about my family?
3. If I could be guaranteed success, what thing would I most want to try?
4. What three things would you most like people to say about you?

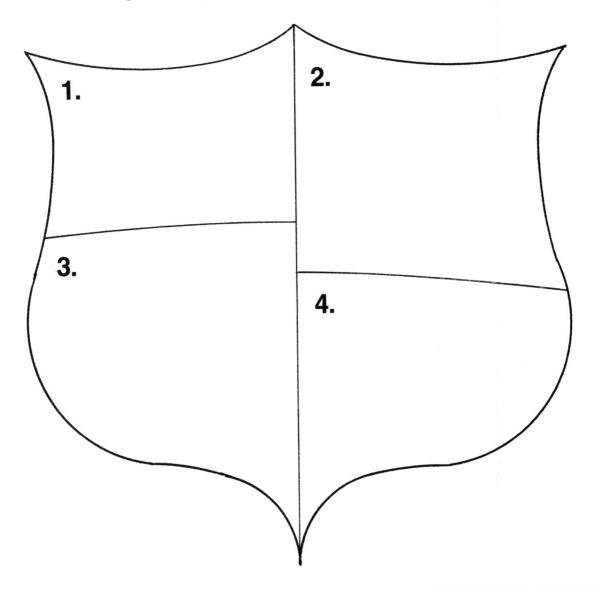

Hearts and Valentines

Most children are familiar with the heart as a symbol of love. But how many children know *why* the heart is associated with affection? How many know that the real heart inside their bodies bears little resemblance to the cutely plump, rosy-red image so popular with doll manufacturers and greeting card companies? In this theme unit, children about to celebrate Valentine's Day will have an opportunity to take a closer look at the bodily organ that is widely recognized as a symbol of love and friendship.

 ## Fast Facts:

○ All animals (this includes humans) have hearts.
○ The heart is a muscle that pumps fresh blood to all the organs and tissues of the body. It is about the size of the owner's fist.
○ It has four parts—two upper chambers, called the right and left auricles, and two lower chambers called the right and left ventricles.
○ The heart has three kinds of blood vessels. The largest—arteries—rush blood away from the heart. Veins, which appear as blue lines under the skin, return blood back to the heart. The smallest—capillaries—help to carry food and oxygen to every cell in the body.
○ The heart pumps blood through the lungs to pick up oxygen and through the kidneys to clean away impurities.
○ The human heart pumps rhythmically at the rate of about 70-80 beats per minute in an adult. Children's heartbeats are slightly faster. Your heart rate can speed up under certain conditions—such as when you are running or jumping, or when you are frightened.
○ You can feel your heart's rhythm by placing your hand on your chest slightly to the left of center.

Getting Started

To begin the unit, ask children to brainstorm all the things they think they know about the human heart. List these things—regardless of their factual accuracy—on a large sheet of chart paper and encourage children to add, change, or delete information as they move through the unit. You may wish to begin each day's lesson by asking children to read what is on the list and suggest additions or changes.

▼ Language Arts

Writing an Expository Paragraph

Ask volunteers to use the encyclopedia or other reference works to research the origins of Valentine's Day, and to peruse legends and fairy tales for references to "the heart." Then briefly review all that has been said about the human heart and the celebration of Valentine's Day. Ask children to think about explaining what Valentine's Day means to someone who has never heard of it. Then encourage students to write one or two sentences stating their main idea.

Allow children to read their sentences to the class and to comment on each others' work. Suggest that they use their sentences as the beginning of a paragraph about the meaning of Valentine's Day. Provide time for children to share their writing with their classmates.

▼ Reading

Looking for Books About the Heart

For more information on the heart and its functions, encourage children to find these and other books in the library.

Your Heart and Blood by Leslie Jean LeMaster (Children's Press)

The Magic School Bus Inside the Human Body by Joanna Cole (Scholastic)

Blood and Guts: A Working Guide to Your Own Insides by Linda Allison (Little, Brown)

After children have read their books, ask them to write down one fact about the heart they did not know before. Have them exchange facts with a partner.

As an additional activity, encourage children to form small groups and improvise short skits based on the experiences of Miss Frizzle (of *The Magic School Bus*) in the heart. Children can conduct their own "journeys" into the heart or travel through some other organ of the body.

▼ Science

Finding Arteries, Veins, and Capillaries

Children may enjoy using a mirror to look under their tongues for thick red arteries, thick blue veins, or thin hair-like capillaries.

More advanced students can find their arteries by locating their pulse points. Remind children that arteries are the largest of the blood vessels. Although arteries lie deep within the body, they come close to the surface in certain spots—such as the wrist and the neck. It is at these points—called pulse points—that one can actually feel the blood pulsing. When a doctor "takes your pulse," she or he is trying to see how your heart is doing. Encourage children to take each others' pulses and to count the number of beats per minute while a subject is sitting down and then jumping in place. Ask children to infer what happens to the heart during strenuous exercise.

 Health

Keeping Hearts Healthy

Ask children to recall what happened to their pulses after jumping in place. What effect do they think this kind of exercise has on the body? Point out to children that certain forms of exercise (aerobic exercise) can help make the heart strong, enabling it to pump more blood to the body's organs and tissues. To illustrate, discuss the way lifting weights can help to build arm and chest muscles, thus enabling a person to lift, carry, do chores, and perform well in sports.

Good for the Heart	Bad for the Heart
aerobic exercise	stress
salads	foods high in cholesterol
proteins	lack of exercise

Most children have heard—whether from the media, their teachers, or parents—about the importance of building a healthy heart. As an activity, have the class brainstorm a list of things that are good and bad for the heart. Children may enjoy creating and illustrating their own posters using their list. You may use this list as a model.

Art

Making a Liquid Starch and Paper Valentine

Children can work in groups with drawing paper, red crepe paper or tissue paper, and liquid starch. (Spray starch is not thick enough, but a thin flour-and-water paste could also serve.) Write these steps on the chalkboard and discuss them:

1. Fold a sheet of white drawing paper in half to make a valentine card.
2. Crush some crepe paper in bunches or strips to make hearts, flowers, or other figures.
3. Stick the crushed paper on the valentine with the liquid starch. Don't worry about dripping or running.
4. Make the color pink by dipping red paper in liquid and then "sponge" painting all over the card—especially over the drips.
5. Let the valentine dry.
6. Use a black crayon or marker to add details. See if you can use the drips and marks to form people, hearts, flowers, or anything you choose.
7. Write a valentine message and give the card to someone you like a lot.

Art

Making a Pop-Up Valentine

Find out if children are familiar with "pop-up books." Allow them to talk about particular ones they have liked. Then tell them that they are going to make a "pop-up" valentine. Have them do the following:

1. Fold a sheet of construction paper in half.
2. Cut out a large heart shape.
3. Cut out a thin strip of paper and fold it down at both ends.

4. Paste one end to the inside of the folded paper and the other end to the heart shape.

5. Think of someone who likes to laugh. Write a two-line rhyme for that person and print it on the valentine.

Math

Making and Using a Line Graph

On the chalkboard, draw a line graph like the one on the activity sheet on page 87. On any Monday, ask children to estimate how many minutes they will spend that day walking, running, playing games, or engaging in some other form of physical activity. Give children a few minutes to perform the calculations. Have them record their active times for each of the five days of the school week. Ask them to put a dot in the appropriate place in the column for each day, and connect the dots with lines. As students record their activities, model the procedure for them by using the graph you drew on the chalkboard. On the following Friday, have children complete their line graphs and tell which day was their most active and why.

Point out that not only is exercise is beneficial to the heart, it increases strength, agility, the ability to think clearly, and even improves one's mood. Ask children if they think they could benefit from more exercise. What are some things they can do? Hand out extra copies of the activity sheet on page 87 to children and encourage them to chart their exercise progress from week to week.

Social Studies

Making the Heart/Valentine Connection

Tell children that the brain has different parts, each of which is responsible for a certain aspect of human activity—such as speech, movement, physical sensation, and the emotions. Ask children to name the different emotions with which they are familiar, especially those that have to do with friendliness, affection, and love.

Pose the following question to children and allow them to voice their responses: "If the brain is where we feel love and affection—and the heart is basically a blood pump—why then do we associate Valentine's Day with the heart rather than with the brain?" Tell children that the heart has been a universal symbol of love and devotion throughout history. Folktales, poems, and fairy tales are filled with the symbol of the heart. Mention such expressions as "I give you my heart," "You are always in my heart," "I love you with my whole heart," and ask children to suggest others they know.

Name: _____

Line Graphing My Exercise Time

TIME	DAYS				
	Monday	Tuesday	Wednesday	Thursday	Friday
4 Hrs.					
3 Hrs. 45 Min.					
3 Hrs. 30 Min.					
3 Hrs. 15 Min.					
3 Hrs.					
2 Hrs. 45 Min.					
2 Hrs. 30 Min.					
2 Hrs. 15 Min.					
2 Hrs.					
1 Hr. 45. Min.					
1 Hr. 30 Min.					
1 Hr. 15 Min.					
1 Hr.					
45 Min.					
30 Min.					
15 Min.					

Hr. = Hour
Min. = Minute

Tools and Simple Machines

Creative thinking and problem solving are the keys to this unit in which the children craft toys and enjoy experiments based on tools and simple machines.

 Fast Facts

○ No matter how complex or powerful a machine is, it is made up of one or more of the following six simple machines: inclined plane, lever, pulley, screw, wedge, wheel-and-axle.
○ Tools and machines usually make work easier.
○ Tools and machines cannot work alone. They need some kind of "power source" (people, heat, air, water, chemicals, or electricity) to make them work.
○ Power tools are tools that have been motorized.
○ Some tools are machines, but others are not machines.
○ We use different tools and machines for different jobs in different places. We have household tools and machines, office tools and machines, gardening tools and machines, etc.

 Getting Started

Invite students to bring in something they made outside of school. Place the homemade objects together on a display table. Allow time for students to "show 'n tell" their handiwork. Encourage students to recount the steps and the tools or machines needed to complete their projects. Also, have students tell about any frustrating moments they experienced during construction as well as any pride they felt in accomplishing what they did.

Ask the children to describe why we have tools and machines. Help students to understand the difference between tools and machines. (Tools are hand-held instruments used to make a job easier, while machines are devices with two or more moving or unmoving parts that usually make work easier.)

Print the following list on the chalkboard. Have students decide if each item is a machine or a tool:

car	hair dryer
pencil	radio
television	scissors
eraser	crock pot
vacuum cleaner	microwave oven
drill	video cassette recorder
elevator	ruler
washing machine	screw
rake	paintbrush
computer	

Reading

Students will enjoy these books about tools and machines.

Cards for Kids: Games, Tricks, and Amazing Facts by Elin McCoy (Macmillan)

Easy-to-Make Water Toys That Really Work by Mary and Dewey Blocksma (Simon & Schuster)

Experiments, Puzzles, and Games: Exploring Electricity by Sandra Markle (Atheneum)

Paper Airplanes to Make and Fly by Jim Razzi (Scholastic)

Paper Tricks by Florence Temko (Scholastic)

Physics for Every Kid by Janice Van Cleave (Wiley)

Sports Mazes by Vladimir Koziakin (Scholastic)

Encourage volunteers to look for ideas in the books, compare them to projects they've already done, and suggest ways to combine new and old knowledge to make a toy or game. After reading about simple machines, have students locate concrete examples of each such as:

○ Inclined plane—a playground slide
○ Lever—a seesaw
○ Pulley—a flag and flagpole mechanism
○ Screw—jar lid
○ Wedge—door stop
○ Wheel-and-axle—bicycle tire mechanism

Technology

Inclined Planes Raceway

Show children various examples of inclined planes such as a playground slide and a loading ramp. Provide students with supplies such as boards, paper towel rolls, boxes, blocks and masking tape. Challenge students to use the supplies to make their own inclined planes.

Show students how the inclined planes can be turned into a raceway game using miniature cars, marbles, balls and wads of paper or foil.

After the groups meet, plan, and construct their raceways, have them demonstrate the results to the class.

Ask:

How might you make the racers go faster? Slower? Come to a stop? Do some materials make better racers than others? Why? What kinds of competition could you hold?

 Observation and Design

Mini-Playgrounds

After visiting a playground, children may work in pairs to construct miniature playgrounds featuring a number of simple machines. Spools, tinker toys, shoe boxes, pencils, dowels, clay, string, tape, glue, and paints will be some of the items the children will find useful in attempting to reconstruct playground equipment.

 Thinking Skills

Wheel-and-Axle Walk

Take children on a walk around the school building and the neighborhood. Challenge children to find as many examples of wheels and axles as they can. If possible, photograph the examples, mount on a large piece of oaktag, and label. Ask children to predict how many wheels-and-axles they might find at home. Then, have children do an actual at-home survey and bring the results to school to share.

 Technology

Playground Pulley Play

Visit the school custodian to borrow a pulley, some rope and a bucket. On the playground, have students fill the bucket with water or stones. Tie one end of the rope to the full bucket. Have students take turns lifting the bucket. Then, suspend the pulley from a high point on the playground (such as from the swing set or from the jungle gym), thread the loose end of the rope through the pulley. Have children take turns pulling on the rope in an attempt to lift the bucket. How did the addition of the pulley change the work load? Have the children speculate why lifting the bucket with the help of the pulley seems easier.

 Physics

Gaining Leverage With Levers

Divide your class into pairs of almost equal weight. Have partners take turns trying to lift each other up. Then, take students to a playground. Show students how a seesaw is an example of a lever. Have partners sit opposite each other on the seesaw. How easy is it for partners to lift each other up with the aide of a seesaw lever? Ask students to explain how and why the work load seemed to change with the addition of a lever. Can they think of any other practical uses for levers? (Hint: If students are unable to think of any ways levers are used, have them interview family members to find examples from around their homes.)

Eye-Hand Coordination

Jar Lid Race

Provide students with a variety of jars with screw-on lids. Inform students that a screw is really an inclined plane wrapped around a core (as in the case of a screw) or a rim (as in the case of a jar lid). Place the lids into a bag and challenge children to match the correct lid to the correct jar and to screw all the lids in place. After students have had a chance to practice, challenge them to attempt to screw the lids on the jars as fast as they can. Keep track of each student's time. Students may decide to be in competition with themselves or each other for the fastest times possible.

Variation: Repeat this activity with a bag of assorted nuts and bolts students must sort and match.

Graphing

Simple Machine Scavenger Hunt

Provide students with copies of the activity sheet on page 92. Ask students to use the sheet to draw one example of each of the simple machines featured. Sheets may be used when students take class walks, or for an at-home activity. Completed sheets may be used to compile a "Simple Machine Graph." Have students cut sheets apart on the lines and glue each example to the correct category on a craft paper chart. See how many different examples of each simple machine type the class can post.

Career Awareness

Tools of the Trade

Cut pictures of machines and tools from mail order catalogs. Glue pictures onto index cards. Place cards into a shoe box. Have students take turns drawing a card from the box and acting out using the machine or tool as the other students try to guess what's pictured on the card.

Variation: For each machine or tool card, supply a matching "career card" featuring a worker who uses the machine or tool. Students must match the machine and tool cards to the career cards. Make the game self-checking, by placing corresponding numbers on the reverse side of each pair of cards.

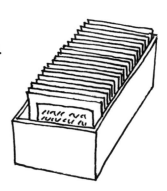

Name:

Tools and Simple Machines

inclined plane

lever

pulley

screw

wedge

wheel-and-axle

Fairy Tales

No matter what reading level or age (and whether they'll admit it or not), most children and adults love hearing and re-hearing Fairy Tales. This unit will bring the magic of Fairy Tales into your classroom.

 Getting Started

To introduce the unit, read aloud this retelling of a little-known Grimm Brothers fairy tale, "The Queen Bee."

Once there were two cruel and reckless brothers who roamed the earth causing trouble wherever they went. One day, their younger brother Witling left home to look for them and bring them back.

Now when Witling found his brothers, they laughed and jeered at him and called him a simpleton. But Witling decided to stay with them, if only to keep them out of trouble. As the three brothers walked along, they came upon an ant hill. The two older brothers stomped and kicked as the terrified ants scurried off, carrying their babies with them. "Stop!" cried Witling. "Leave these innocent creatures alone! I cannot bear to see you harm them!"

So the three brothers went on further until they came to a lake where ducks were swimming peacefully. The older brothers plunged into the water, preparing to capture some ducks for their evening feast. "Stop!" cried Witling. "Leave these innocent creatures alone! I cannot bear to see you harm them!"

So the three brothers continued on their way until they saw—high up in a tree—a Queen Bee's nest overflowing with honey. The two older brothers built a smoking fire at the foot of the tree and the gasping bees began to choke. "Stop!" cried Witling. "I cannot bear to see you harm them!"

Bye and bye the brothers came to an enchanted castle inside of which a princess and all her royal family had been turned to stone. Strangely, however, there was one old man who was quite alive. He gave them food and drink, and then he said to the brothers, "If you can perform three tasks, the spell of the castle will be broken and all within it will be yours. But take care," the old man continued, "for if you do not succeed, you, too, will be turned to stone."

The first task was to go out into the forest and find, by sunset, a thousand diamonds belonging to the princess. But when the eldest brother could only find one hundred, he was instantly turned to stone. The following day, the middle brother undertook the task, but he fared no better and was also turned to stone.

(Continued)

And so it was Witling's turn. He went into the forest with a heavy heart. He searched until it was almost sunset and then he sat down on a rock and wept. Suddenly, the Ant King appeared with his five thousand subjects—all of whom had been saved by Witling. The ants scurried through the forest and in no time at all heaped 1000 diamonds before the weeping boy. So Witling did not turn to stone—at least, not that night.

The following morning, the old man told Witling of his second task. "Go to the lake," the old man said. "Somewhere at the bottom is a key to the chamber where the princess sleeps. Recover it and bring it back." Witling went to the lake with a heavy heart until he met his old friends, the ducks. They dived down into the water and came up again, dropping the key at the amazed boy's feet.

Now the third task was the most difficult of all. In the sleeping chamber, there was not one princess—but three! "They look exactly alike," the old man said to Witling "but only one has a kind heart. It was she who had eaten honey before she was turned to stone. Identify that princess and all will be yours." Witling thought and thought but could not tell how to choose the right princess. Just then, the Queen Bee—whose nest Witling had saved—flew in through the window. Going from one princess to the other, the Queen Bee lit on the mouth that tasted of honey. "It is this princess who has the kind heart!" whispered Witling.

Slowly, as if waking from a deep sleep, the princesses and all the castle stirred and came alive. Witling's brothers, who had also awakened, realized for the first time that goodness always triumphs. They hung their heads and turned to walk away.

"Stop!" said Witling. "I cannot bear to see you go!" So the brothers stayed at the castle and mended their ways. No one knows for sure if they did it out of goodness—or because the ants, the ducks, and the Queen Bee were watching.

Some fairy tales—like the one above, were told to teach a lesson. Ask children to guess what lesson "The Queen Bee" teaches. (Hint: the answer is in the next-to-the-last paragraph!)

☑ Language Arts

Round-Robin Storytelling

Suggest that children tell the story of "The Queen Bee" in their own words. First have them sit in circle formation. Ask the first child to begin with the introduction and to stop after a few sentences—allowing the next child to pick up where the first left off. Give each child in the circle a chance to tell a part of the story, and allow them to continue until the story is completed. Remind children that they are free to embellish the story in their own way.

▽ Social Studies

Comparing Stories from Different Cultures

Fairy tales and folk tales are stories handed down from generation to generation. Although some of these stories were eventually written down, they are considered to be part of a people's oral tradition. Fairy tales and folk tales were important to people as a way to transmit knowledge and culture, to explain the mysteries of the world, and to instill moral values. Every region of the world has its own fairy tales. Sometimes you can find a fairy tale from a particular region of the world that seems very similar to a fairy tale from another region of the world. This is because groups of people carried their stories with them as they traveled from place to place.

To illustrate, locate several versions of the Red Riding Hood story including the Chinese version, *Lon Po-Po* by Ed Young (Scholastic). Other versions include *Little Red Riding Hood* by Karen Schmidt (Scholastic), *Red Riding Hood* by Beatrice Schenk de Regniers (Atheneum), and *Red Riding Hood* by James Marshall (Scholastic). Read the stories aloud to children, or ask volunteers to read them aloud. After all versions have been read, ask children to compare and contrast the versions. You may want to list the similarities and differences in chart form.

▽ Reading

Reading Fairy Tales

The following are beautifully illustrated books of fairy tales:

Aladdin and the Wonderful Lamp by Carol Carrick (Scholastic)

Puss in Boots illustrated by Fred Marcellino (Farrar, Straus, Giroux)

Rip Van Winkle by Freya Littledale (Scholastic)

Rumpelstiltskin by Edith Tarcov (Scholastic)

The Seven Chinese Brothers by Margaret Mahy (Scholastic)

The Swineherd by Hans Christian Andersen (Lothrop)

The Three Billy-Goats Gruff by Ellen Appleby (Scholastic)

The Tinderbox retold by Peggy Thomson (Simon & Schuster)

▽ Creative Writing and Language Arts

Writing or Telling Your Own Fairy Tale

Children will enjoy writing—or telling—their own fairy tales based on "The Queen Bee." Give each student a copy of the activity sheet on page 97. Explain to children that they can use the sheet to give them ideas, or to provide a framework for their own ideas. Children may choose to work independently or in pairs.

Allow children the option of writing their stories or telling them to the class. (Younger students may want to tell them.) Whatever the method, make sure to provide ample time for children to share what they've written with their classmates.

▼ Creative Writing and Art

Making Fairy Tale Big Books

Children may be familiar with Big Books from their classroom activities. Suggest that children make their own fairy tale Big Books. They can retell a known fairy tale, using ideas from the activity sheet or make up an entirely new story. Before they begin, ask the class to brainstorm kinds of tasks that might be involved in the making of a Big Book; for example, taking notes on story ideas, drafting the story, making editorial changes, laying out the pages, printing, and illustrations. Write these tasks on the chalkboard.

To make a six-page book, take three large rectangular sheets of oak tag and make creases in the center of each sheet for a binding. (See illustration below.) The innermost spread should have a binding 1/2 inch in width, the middle spread should have a binding 3/4 inch in width, and the outer spread should have a binding 1 inch in width. Paste the spines of the inner spreads onto the bindings of the spreads underneath it.

Allow children to form small groups. Have the groups meet in planning sessions and assign tasks to each of their members, making sure each member has something to do that suits his or her interests and abilities.

When the books are complete, have a volunteer from each group read aloud and display the books to the class.

▼ Art and Creative Dramatics

Putting on a Puppet-Show

Children will enjoy making their own puppets and putting on a puppet show using well-known or original fairy tales.

First, tell children that there are certain things they'll need to consider when they plan their puppet-show—for example, what kinds of puppets they want to use; how they want to stage their show; whether or not they want music or sound effects—and if so, what kind; what story they want to use; and who will play each part.

Help children brainstorm ideas. Suggestions for puppets include sock puppets, finger puppets, or puppets made of ice-cream sticks. You may wish to create a "stage" out of a tabletop or you may wish to build a stage using cardboard and swatches of material as curtains. Point out to children that it is better to choose a fairy tale with few characters. In addition, advise them to use a plot outline to guide them as they move through the scenes.

When you feel the children are sufficiently prepared, help them to form groups of four or five and allow them to meet in their groups. Depending on the elaborateness of the production, you may wish to have groups meet several more times before they perform their plays for the class.

Write Your Own Fairy Tale

Color in a dot beside one in each list or write your own idea.

The characters are:
- ○ 3 brothers
- ○ 3 sisters
- ○ 3 friends
- ○ _____

Where the characters go:
- ○ to the forest
- ○ to a lake or river
- ○ to the mountains
- ○ _____

What the characters find there:
- ○ 3 snakes
- ○ 6 ferocious dragons
- ○ 9 one-eyed, mud-spitting creatures
- ○ _____

What happens first? Write it here.

_____

_____

What happens next? Write it here.

_____

_____

What happens last? Write it here.

_____

_____

Now use these notes to write and draw your story on other paper.

_____

Picasso

Pablo Picasso is arguably the most famous artist of the Twentieth century-maybe of all time. Though his boundless talent would eventually earn him more money and recognition than any other artist had ever earned during his or her own lifetime, Picasso's schooldays were not happy: He had great difficulty with most academic subjects. (His artistic talent, however, was recognized from a young age.) A study of Picasso can help your students realize that there are many different ways of excelling.

Fast Facts

○ Born October 25, 1881, at Malaga, Spain. He died 91 years later, on April 8, 1973. Although he was born in Spain and was of Spanish descent, from 1904 onward he lived in France, and is considered a French artist.

○ Picasso's art often reflected his emotional and financial state. The paintings of his "Blue Period" (1901-1904) were done while he lived in poverty amid poor beggars and weary-looking workers. During 1905 and 1906, his luck began to change. His work was becoming recognized, and he was happily in love. The paintings done during this time are called his "Rose Period" works.

○ Guernica, one of the landmarks of his career, was comissioned for the Spanish Pavilion at the World's Fair in Paris. It depicted the destruction of the town of Guernica by German bombing.

○ Picasso produced over 20,000 objects in his lifetime, including drawings, paintings, sculptures, and ceramics. He also wrote poetry and at least one play, and designed costumes for ballets. He also made "readymades," sculptures composed of found objects which Picasso combined in unusual ways, like the bicycle seat and handlebars which he put together to look like a bull's head (called, appropriately, *Bull*.)

○ With his friend and fellow artist, Georges Braque, Picasso invented Cubism, in which everyday objects are depicted as masses of geometric shapes.

▷ Getting Started

   To begin, locate one example of Picasso's work in an art book or an encyclopedia. Choose one painting to share with the class. Find a picture of the same subject in a magazine or newspaper, and show it to the children, too. (Possible subjects: a chicken, a man playing a guitar, circus acrobats, a deck of playing cards, a woman, a bullfight. Show both pictures to the children and have them discuss similarities, differences, and their reactions. Which do they prefer-the realistic magazine picture, or Picasso's version? Ask: Do they think Picasso drew the way he did because he couldn't do realistic work? Encourage the children to discuss the reasons they think Picasso may have had for painting the way he did. What different feelings do the children get from the realistic pictures and the abstract or cubist ones? What different kinds of things do the different pictures make them think of? Encourage research and discussion. You may want to chart student preferences on the chalkboard, under the headings, "I prefer realistic art because:" and "I prefer Picasso's art because:" Students may write a paragraph or essay supporting their opinion.

Reading

Learning About Picasso

Locate and display magazine articles, chapters from art books, and books about Picasso in a classroom "Picasso Center." Choose some selections about Picasso's childhood and others about his work to read aloud. This may be where you want to introduce some of the "Fast Facts" as background. Some suggested titles to share with the children:

A Weekend With Picasso by Florian Rodari (Rizzoli)

Pablo Picasso by Ibi Lepscky (Barrons)

Pablo Picasso: The Man and the Image by Richard B. Lyttle (Atheneum)

Pablo Picasso: Master of Modern Art by Miranda Smith (Creative Education)

Pablo Picasso: The Minotaur by Daniele Giraudy (Abrams)

Math

Identifying Geometric Shapes

Invite volunteers to the chalkboard to draw examples of squares, circles, rectangles and triangles.

Have the children identify these shapes in the reproductions of Picasso's paintings you've collected, and tell them that this painting style, which Picasso helped to invent, is called "Cubism." The subjects were often arrangements of items such as bowls, cups, or fruits, known as "still life." Invite the children to create their own cubism-inspired artworks using geometric shapes. Provide empty wine bottles, fruit, bowls, or flowers for them to draw or paint. Have children sign their work and display it in the "Picasso Center."

Art

Making a Collage

Picasso used newsprint, wallpaper, stamps, and parts of other pictures to make collages. He juxtaposed the items in a way that didn't always seem to make sense to others, but that pleased Picasso. You may be able to locate an example of one of Picasso's collages in one of your reference materials. If so, show it to your students, then provide them with glue, bits of cloth, string, labels from canned food, popsicle sticks, and other "junk" they can use to make their own collages. Encourage children to sign and entitle their collages before displaying.

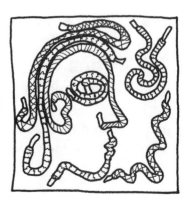

Painting a Period

Talk about and show examples of Picasso's blue and rose periods. Remind the children that those paintings of the rose period were happy ones depicting acrobats and other circus performers. Have the children use black pencil to draw figures for a blue or rose period. Then have them color in the figures with red or blue watercolors.

 ## Science and Art

Color Mixing

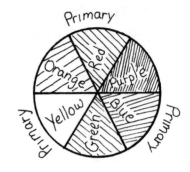

Picasso said, "When I don't have blue, I use red." Your students can use unusual colors in their paintings, too, creating a blue tree, or a yellow sky, if they don't have the "correct" color. Or, they can experiment with color mixing using tempera paint. The primary colors, blue, red, and yellow, can be combined to create all the other colors your students will ever need for their artwork. Adding white paint to a color students have mixed will give a lighter tint. Adding black paint to a color will give a darker shade.

 ## Social Studies

Recycling Junk into Art

Talk about the need to recycle. Ask parents to send in the contents of their kitchen "junk drawers," and bring in junk of your own. Start a junk drive in school for discarded objects that have lost their usefulness, and collect them in your classroom, in a large cardboard box labeled "Art Supplies." When you've collected enough, invite your students to select items to combine to create "readymades," just like Picasso did when he created "Bull."

 ## Feelings

Building Self-Esteem

Picasso's father was a painter and art teacher. He liked to paint pigeons. When Picasso was only 13 years old, his father went out for a walk one evening, and invited his son to finish a painting on which he had been working. Picasso finished painting the pigeons' feet, and when his father returned, he saw how much better his son's work was than his own. Encourage students to think about, discuss, write about, or illustrate the things they do around the house or in the classroom that help the older people in their lives.

Writing

Other Art Forms

Picasso's genius extended to the written word. He found grammar and punctuation difficult, and so wrote free verse. Copy and distribute the worksheet on page 101, so individual students can use it to write "Picasso Poems."

Picasso Poetry

You've learned a lot about Pablo Picasso. Now use what you've learned to write a poem about Picasso on the lines below. Use the first letter on the line as the first letter of each line of your poem. You can write just one word on each line, a few words, or a complete sentence. When you're finished, share your poem with the class.

P _____

A _____

B _____

L _____

O _____

P _____

I _____

C _____

A _____

S _____

S _____

O _____

Children From Other Countries

America is unique in that it is home to people from every nation on the earth. Your students will understand this, as well as appreciating the contributions of all ethnic groups in building America, as they study this unit on children from other countries.

 Fast Facts

The following are descriptions of the countries and cultures whose people have immigrated to the United States in the recent past. You may want to read some of these to pique interest before the children choose a country for their group work.

○ **Cuba** This Spanish-speaking island is only 100 miles away from the coast of Florida. The government in 1992 is one of the last bastions of communism in the world. It is mountainous with beautiful beaches. At the age of twelve, many Cuban children are sent to boarding schools, where they study in the morning and work the crops in the field for the rest of the day. Sugar cane is the most important crop.

○ **Ethiopia** This country is situated on the continent of Africa. Its people are poor and plagued by drought, political wars, sickness, and starvation. There are many groups in the United States, including children, who are active in performing charitable works to relieve the sufferings of the Ethiopian people.

○ **Haiti** Many of the citizens were brought to this Caribbean island as slaves from Africa. The country was once owned by the French, and that is why Haitian people speak French to this day.

○ **Ireland** This European country has sent many of its people to America for over a hundred years. It is a beautiful green place of rolling hills and valleys. Much of our folklore of elves and leprechauns comes from this country.

○ **Russia** This country, once part of the old Soviet Union, has a fascinating history. Much Russian literature and music is studied in the United States. This is a country currently working for change and a democratic way of life. The children in Russia study very hard and have a strong family social life.

○ **India** Cities in India are modern and filled with cultural advantages, but some children in the cities and countrysides live in mud huts with no furniture. Within the country there are fourteen main languages and over 700 other languages and dialects.

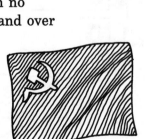

▶ Getting Started

Help students understand that the majority of people living in the United States came from other places in the world, or have ancestors who came from other places. Tell the children that many other countries are made up mostly of people of the same ethnic and cultural background but that the United States is often called "the Melting Pot" or the "Salad Bowl" because it is a melting together or combination of many customs, cultures and ethnic backgrounds.

Together with the children, look up the definition of "ancestors," "immigrant" and "immigration." Older students may also learn the definition of "ethnic," "nationality" and "culture." Provide each student with a copy of the activity sheet on page 109. Ask the children to use the sheet to interview family members in order to discover and record their family's country or countries of origin. If possible, children should also record the approximate dates of their ancestors' immigration to the United States, how they traveled, and the reasons for their move. Back in class, transfer as much research as possible to an "immigration time line." Undated immigration information may be recorded on mini-posters and displayed surrounding the time line. Have students give brief oral presentations recounting their research.

Ancestors –
Relatives who lived long ago.

Nationality –
The country a person's ancestors come from.

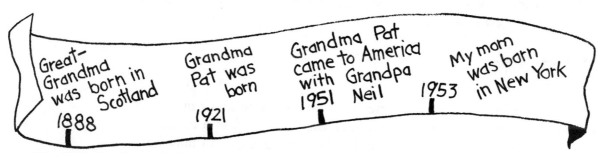

Great-Grandma was born in Scotland 1888

Grandma Pat was born 1921

Grandma Pat came to America with Grandpa Neil 1951

My mom was born in New York 1953

You may also have children label small construction paper flags with their names and pin the flags to a world map indicating their ancestors' countries of origin as well as their own country of origin. (Use one color flag for students' countries of origin and another color flag for their ancestors' countries of origin.)

Mario

Isabel

▽ Art

Making Travel Posters

Ask your local travel agent to lend or donate some travel posters to your classroom. Also, select a number of foreign travel brochures to bring to school. After spending class time reviewing the details of the brochures and posters, have children use markers and tempera paints on oaktag to create travel posters representing their ancestors' countries of origin, or other places of interest. Hang the posters up around the classroom and allow children time to share posters with classmates.

☑ Social Studies

Listening and Asking Questions About Other Cultures

Invite U.S. immigrants (parents, students, colleagues, etc.) to your class to talk about life in their country of origin. Encourage visitors to bring and share any photos, artifacts or related news clippings that may help enhance their presentations. Help students prepare for each visitor by generating a list of questions regarding work, play, diet, language and education. Follow-up each visit by having students make posters comparing and contrasting aspects of the foreign lifestyle with their own.

☑ Language Arts

Listening and Expressing an Opinion

Locate *Making a New Home in America* by Maxine Rosenberg (Lothrop). Illustrated with photographs of children who emigrated from various countries including Japan, South Africa, Guyana, Cuba, India, and Vietnam, the book describes the humorous and challenging personal experiences of the children's adjustment to life in America. Ask the children to imagine what it must feel like to be an immigrant. Ask students to draw on their own experiences in order to recount how it feels to be newcomers to a situation. Have students brainstorm a list of ways they might help a newcomer feel welcome. Also, have students generate a list of ways they may help themselves feel more confident in new situations. Refer to the lists when a new student joins the class or when students are preparing to enter new experiences.

☑ Social Studies

Research

Have the class decide on several countries they would like to know more about. Divide students into small groups and have each group select a country to research. Depending on the age and ability level of your group, you may want to help students in each group divide up the research responsibilities. Student research should focus on aspects such as:

○ geography of the country
○ family traditions
○ clothing
○ arts and entertainment
○ food
○ education

Help each group record their findings in a collaborative booklet (comprised of individual essays and illustrations bound together). Also consider having each group prepare and present an audio-visual research component such as a dance, a song, a poem or a folktale reflective of their country's culture.

Reading

Learning About Other Cultures

Help students locate companion copies of books that are printed in two languages. Here are some suggestions:

Bilingual:

Arroz Con Leche: Popular Sons and Rhymes from Latin America by Lulu Delacre (Scholastic)

Babar's French Lessons by Laurent De Brunhoff (Random House)

Count Your Way Through Israel by Jim Haskins (Carolrhoda)

Historia De Babar by Jean De Brunhoff (Ediciones Alfaguara S. A.)

Moja Means One by Muriel Feelings (Dial)

Tortillitas Para Mama and Other Nursery Rhymes selected by Griego, Bucks, Gilbert, and Kimball (Holt)

In addition to bilingual books, encourage the children to look for books about the lives of immigrants such as:

Abiyoyo by Pete Seeger (Scholastic)

Abuela by Arthur Dorros (Dutton)

All-of-Kind Family by Sydney Taylor (Follett)

Angel Child, Dragon Child by Michele Maria Surat (Scholastic)

Berchnick by Esther Silverstein Blanc (Volcano Press)

Hill of Fire by Thomas P. Lewis (Scholastic)

I Hate English by Ellen Levine (Scholastic)

Immigrant Kids by Russell Freedom (Dutton)

Red Bird of Ireland by Sondra Gordon (Atheneum)

The Road from Home: The Story of an Armenian Girl by David Kherdian (Greenwillow)

FACES the Magazine About People is filled with pictures, photographs, stories, and articles. Each month, the entire magazine is devoted to one featured country or culture.

Art

Making a Water Puppet from Vietnam

Share the book *Look What We've Brought You From Vietnam* by Phyllis Shalant (Julian Messner). In addition to stories, games, and recipes, there are crafts, including the making of a water puppet similar to the one described below. It is said that for thousands of years in Vietnam, water puppet shows were given in which puppeteers

stood waist-deep in lake water with a floating matt or reeds as the stage. They manipulated the puppets with rods.

To make a water puppet, give the children copies of the activity sheet on page 108, and pieces of stiff cardboard. Help them follow the directions on the activity sheet, and manipulate the puppets, using rods made from pipe cleaners, wires, drinking straws, old chopsticks, or any other items.

To present a water play, have volunteers cover a table with bunched-up blue crepe paper suggesting waves on a lake. Some children will want to read more about Vietnam, and make their puppet shows reflect what they have read.

 ## Music

Singing and Dancing

Invite family members and friends of the children to come in and teach a song or dance from their country. Find musical recordings in the library to play as the children work on art and other projects. Three good recordings are:

"Dances of the World's Peoples," Vol. 2, Music from France, Italy, Ireland, and Spain (Folkways).

"Dances of the World's Peoples," Vol. 4, Music from Armenia, Caucasia, Greece, Israel, and Turkey (Folkways).

"Latin American Children's Game Songs" by Henrietta Yurchenco (Folkways).

Geography

Finding Out How Land Affects the Way People Live

The children can use the classroom library to find topographical maps. They may then work in pairs to find information and present oral reports to answer questions such as these:

○ What is the land like? Is it flat, hilly, mountainous, a desert?
○ How do the people use their special kind of land for building homes, growing food, traveling, providing for recreation and play?

Language Arts

Role Playing

After the children have explored several other countries, talk about specific differences children from those countries might find when moving to the United States. Help them role play what it might be like to be a child from a foreign country experiencing the following school scenarios:

○ first day at school
○ first classroom celebration, such as Halloween, Thanksgiving, Valentine's Day, a classmate's birthday, etc.
○ first experience at playing unfamiliar playground games
○ first attempts to understand and speak a new language

After each pretend scenario is acted out, have the children talk about how the new child felt and how they could possibly ease such a transition.

Reading

Learning Rhymes From Other Countries

Locate a copy of *Street Rhymes Around the World* edited by Jane Yolen (Boyds Mills Press). After you and the children have shared some of the rhymes, compile a booklet of rhymes common to the children in the class. Be sure to include information telling where the children in class first learned the rhymes.

Language Arts

Listening and Reporting From Home

Remind the children that their ancestors came from another place a long time ago. Read the book and show the pictures in *Ellis Island, New Hope in a New Land* by William Jacobs (Scribner's). After discussing the book, have the children ask at home about their family's immigrant experiences. Some may want to give a talk or draw a picture to tell about it.

 Music

Listening to a Singing Story

Tell the children that when people come from other countries they bring their stories and music with them. One example is the operas that originated in Italy, France, Germany, and other countries. The opera *Aida* by Giuseppe Verdi is an exciting introduction to this art form that uses music to tell stories. After a first playing of the music, tell the children that the opera *Aida* is often presented with live camels and elephants. Mention that there is an outdoor theater in Italy that presents the opera in that way. To help explain the story behind the opera, locate the book *Aida* by Leontyne Price (Harcourt Brace Jovanovich). Consider asking your music teacher to help students put one or two of their favorite classic or original stories to music.

Making a Vietnamese Water Puppet

Follow these steps:

1. Color and cut out two figures, then paste on stiff cardboard.
2. Tape a dowel or cardboard "rod" to the back of each puppet.
3. Use the puppets to put on a water puppet play.

Name: _____

Children from Other Countries

Immigrant Interview Sheet

Name	Country of Origin	Date of Immigration	Mode of Travel	Reasons for Move

SPRING

Young and Old Together

This unit explores the special bond that exists between children and their grandparents, older relatives, and older friends and neighbors.

 Getting Started

To begin, locate the Caldecott Honor book *When I Was Young in the Mountains* by Cynthia Rylant (Dutton). The book tells the author's story of how she grew up in her grandparent's house in the coal mining region of West Virginia.

Read the book to children. Then ask them to describe the girl's relationship with her grandparents. What parts of the book told them how the girl felt about her grandparents, and how they felt about her?

Then ask children if they have a grandparent, older relative, or older friend with whom they feel a special connection. What kinds of things do they do together?

 Reading

Reading About Young and Old Together

Below is a list of books focusing on the relationship between the young and the old. Divide the class into reading groups according to children's level of reading proficiency. Assign each group a book to read. Have children in each group take turns reading a few pages aloud. When the book is finished, invite one volunteer from each group to present an oral book report to the class.

Mr. Gumpy's Motor Car by John Burningham (Viking). Mr. Gumpy, out for a ride in his vintage convertible, takes along an assortment of children and animals. The text is sparse, uses repetition, and good for young readers. *Mr. Gumpy's Outing* (Holt) is similar, but this time the vehicle is a rowboat.

When I Am Old With You by Angela Johnson (Orchard Books). Told in simple words, this story centers on a small boy who tells his grandfather about all the things they will do when they are old together—such as sit on rocking chairs, look at old family photographs, and take long walks.

Old Henry by Joan Blox (Morrow). The neighborhood is ruined because Old Henry won't fix up his place. But when he moves away, the neighbors miss him—and he misses them.

My Grandma Has Black Hair by Mary Hoffman and Joanna Burroughs (Dial). A little girl sees pictures in books of white-haired grannies knitting, but her grandma has black hair and makes gorilla costumes.

No Friends by James Stevenson (Greenwillow). When his grandchildren complain about their new neighborhood, Grandpa tells an exaggerated tale of how much worse it was in his day. This humorous story is told in easy-to-read cartoons. In *The Worst*

Crab in the World at Crab Beach, the grandchildren listen to another of Grandpa's exaggerated stories.

Uncle Melvin by Daniel Pinkwater (Macmillan). This is the touching story of a young boy's relationship with a beloved uncle who lives in a world of his own. Completely different in tone is *Aunt Lulu* (Macmillan), the title character of which runs a mobile library drawn by fourteen Alaskan huskies wearing sunglasses.

Now One Foot, Now the Other by Tomie de Paola (The Trumpet Club). In this tender story, a devoted grandson shows his love for his stroke-victim grandfather by teaching him to walk in the same way his grandfather once taught him.

Georgia Music by Helen Griffith (Greenwillow). Georgia music is the harmonica music a little girl plays for her old and sick grandfather whenever he misses his Georgia home.

My Grandpa and the Sea by Katherine Orr (Carolrhoda). Set on the Caribbean island of St. Lucia, this book tells the story of a girl's grandfather, who is wise despite the fact that he has never attended school.

 Language Arts

Listening to Real-Life Stories

Invite older members of your community to come to your class and tell stories about what it was like to grow up long ago. Ask them to bring in photographs, old toys or appliances, and other memorabilia to help children compare present-day life to life in the past.

Help children to anticipate the event by discussing what they might like to know about the speaker's life. Help children compile a list of questions they might like to ask, such as:

○ Did you watch TV when you were a kid?
○ What did you do for fun?
○ How was school the same or different?
○ What is the biggest difference between the world of today and the world as it was then?

 Language Arts

Making Books

In a classroom discussion, ask children to describe their favorite older person. Invite them to tell what they know of that person's life, what they like most about being with that person, and a memorable episode in their relationship.

Encourage children to write a draft of a story using these and other reflections. When they have completed their draft, have children show their work to a partner for comments and suggestions. Then have children revise and rewrite their stories onto "book pages"—sheets of blank paper folded in half, covered with construction paper, and stapled or sewn together.

Ask children to create illustrations, give their books titles, and be sure to write the author's name—their own—on the cover of the book. Suggest that children give the books to the person they wrote about, or, alternatively, you might try setting up a table or shelf where the books can be displayed and read by children at their leisure. To encourage a sense of authorship, read several of these books aloud during story time—just as if they were professionally published.

Art and Reading

Drawing a Fantasy Picture

Locate and read aloud one of the following books—or another of your choice—involving a character who has an adventure with a much older person.

Abuela by Arthur Dorros (Dutton)

Grandma and the Pirates by Phoebe Gilman (Scholastic)

Ask children to choose an older person with whom they might like to have a fantastic adventure. Provide each child with a large sheet of drawing paper and have them divide the paper into four parts. In each part, children can draw a picture of one episode of the adventure. When the pictures are completed, invite children to take turns displaying their work and to describe what is happening in each episode of the story.

Social Studies

Learning From an Older Person

Guide children to understand that older people know a lot because they have seen and experienced many things during the course of their lives. Ask children what kinds of things an older person might know more about than a younger person. Then have children suggest activities old and young people could do together—activities that would give younger people a great opportunity to learn from their elders. List children's ideas on the chalkboard. Possible suggestions include:

○ exploring old or ethnic neighborhoods
○ cooking favorite family recipes
○ looking at old family photographs or memorabilia
○ identifying leaves, bugs, rocks, and plants in parks and wilderness areas
○ talking about the way people live now with the way things used to be
○ taking a trip to an art museum, a natural history museum, or the local historical society

Encourage children to ask an older friend or relative to accompany them on one of these activities, or another that seems appealing. Have children share their experiences with the class.

Social Studies

Planning an Intergenerational Party

Suggest an intergenerational classroom party! This would be a great opportunity for children to get to know some of the older people in their community. Encourage each child to invite one person they know over the age of sixty. Ask children to brainstorm plans they need to make in order to ensure that their party is a success. Write children's ideas on the chalkboard. These may include:

○ activities and entertainment (e.g., a talent show)
○ snacks and drinks
○ invitations
○ decorations

Ask children to form committees according to their area of interest or the needs of the class. The committees can meet every day for several successive days until all plans are made.

Social Studies

Community Project

Too often, children and older people in today's society are estranged from one another as groups. This is an arrangement where everybody loses—children are deprived of additional adult attention, role models, and a sense of history and cultural heritage; older people miss companionship, and the opportunity to teach others about what they have learned.

One very meaningful way to help children and older adults interact is to have your class visit a senior citizen center, residence, or nursing home. You may wish to begin the process by locating a nearby senior citizen facility, contacting the director, and discussing several ideas. Depending on the type of facility, you may wish to have children present a play or perform songs and dances; or, alternatively, you may wish to involve children and old people in a cultural activity, field trip, or other type of project. Ideally, visits can be ongoing and relationships between the young and the old can evolve naturally.

For more ideas on how to set up a relationship with a senior citizen facility, see *Kids Care* by Joan Novelli and Beth Chayet (Scholastic).

Social Studies and Math

Completing a Family Time Line

Give each child a copy of the activity sheet on page 117. Tell children that a time line is a method of identifying important events in history by marking them off on a line that represents the passage of time. Guide children to see that time lines are useful for getting information at a glance about what happened over a period of years.

Encourage children to use the time line to mark off important events in the lives of their grandparents and great-grandparents. Children will need to do research to find out information on dates of births, deaths, marriages, immigration, and so on. Time lines can be simple or they can be more elaborate, depending on the abilities of your students. Children will enjoy seeing their time lines displayed on a classroom wall or hallway bulletin board. You may wish to mount a more complete exhibit that includes the time lines as well as other writings and drawings about young and old together.

Name: _____

The People in Your Life Time Line

Put a date in the middle empty squares.
Draw a box where your birth year would be.
Write your name in that box.
Fill in the other years of family, friends, and neighbors.

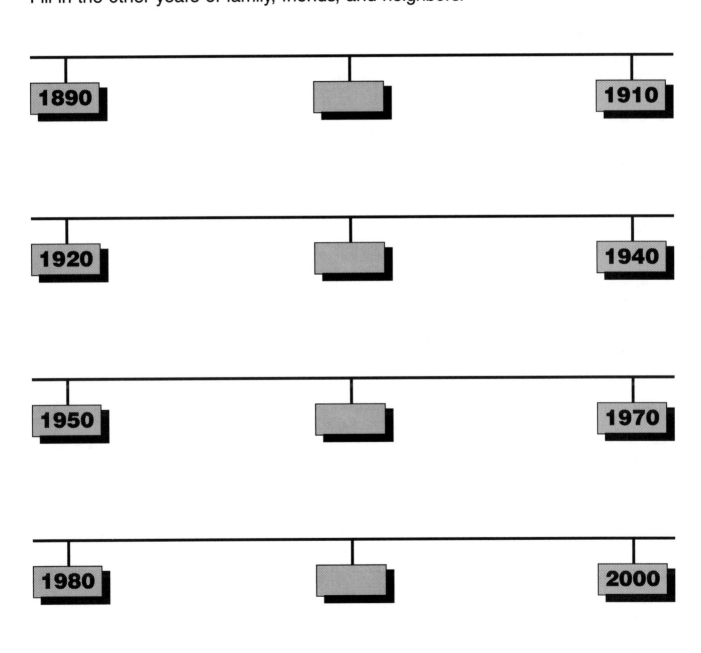

Frogs

Did you know that frogs are everywhere? It's true. Frogs live on farms, in towns, in big cities, in mountains, on grassy plains, and in deserts. So chances are good for your class to observe frogs in the classroom, in books, or in nature.

 Fast Facts

○ Frogs are amphibians (from the Greek, *amphibios*, which means "double life.") The name is appropriate, because frogs start life as water-dwelling vegetarians, and grow up to be carnivorous land-dwellers.

○ They breathe through their skin, which allows them to survive under water or in mud without coming to the surface for air for long periods of time.

○ The process by which a frog changes from an egg, to a tadpole, to an adult frog is called "metamorphosis."

○ In France, where frogs are considered a culinary delicacy, somewhere between 3000 and 4000 tons of frog legs are eaten each year!

○ The croaking sounds frogs make are the way male frogs attract females.

○ Frogs are different from toads, although both come under the scientific grouping "frogs." Toads are fatter, bumpier, drier, have shorter hind legs, and therefore hop, rather than jump, and they spend more time away from water than frogs.

 Getting Started

To begin, create a "Know/Want to Know" chart. After listing what the children already know about frogs, list all the questions children can think of. As the unit progresses and the questions are answered, they can be crossed off or erased. If new questions arise, they can be added.

Reading

Finding Out About Frogs

The following books are available in most libraries, and can be displayed in a classroom "Frog Center."

Discovering Frogs by Douglas Florian (Scribner)

Discovering Toads and Frogs by Mike Linley (Bookwright Press)

The Frog by Margaret Lane (Dial)

Frog and Toad Watching by David Webster (Julian, Messner)

A Frog's Body by Joanna Cole (Morrow)

Slippery Babies/Young Frogs, Toads, and Salamanders, by Ginny Johnston and Judy Cutchins (Morrow)

Frogs, Toads, Lizards, and Salamanders, by Nancy Winslow Parker and Joan Richards Wright (Greenwillow)

 Science

Metamorphosis

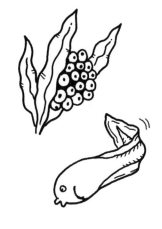

One of the most interesting things about frogs is the dramatic change from tadpole to adult frog. After the female frog lays a clump of eggs in the water, they are fertilized by a male frog. The eggs are surrounded by a soft, jellylike substance, in which the frog embryos develop. When the eggs hatch, tiny tadpoles emerge, with round bodies, tails (in which they store nutrients from the algae they eat), and gills, (through which they breathe, like fish). In time, the tadpole begins to grow hind legs, then front legs. It grows lungs, which replace the gills. The eyes move toward the top of the head and bulge outward.

Gradually, the frog's body absorbs the nutrient-rich tail. The mouth, which was a small hole, becomes a large opening, able to catch large insects. Read about and discuss these changes with your students, then distribute copies of the activity sheet on page 122. Help the children complete it, using the information they've learned in their frog discussions and frog readings. Share the completed activity sheets by displaying them in the "Frog Center."

 Math

Froggie Jumpers

Frogs use their large, powerful hind legs to jump long distances. (You may want to read Mark Twain's *The Jumping Frog of Calaveras County* to your students to illustrate this point.) Your students can use the origami pattern below to create frogs that will jump.

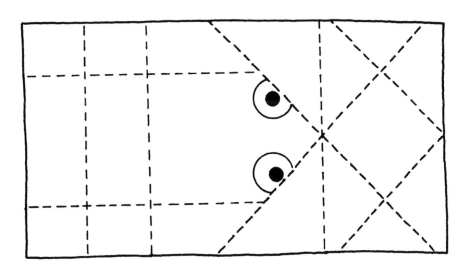

Materials:

For each student:

○ 1 frog pattern
○ 1 index card or 3″ × 5″ piece of paper cut from manila folders

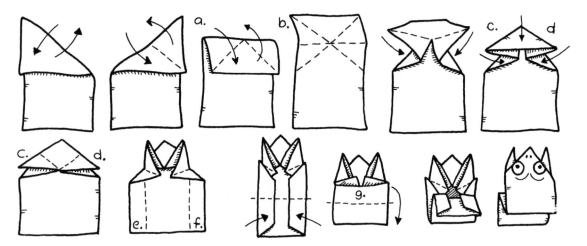

Procedure:

1. Fold top right corner over to left edge, then open.
2. Fold top left corner over to right edge, then open.
3., 4. Fold down top on line AB, then open.
5., 6. Push A and B in and down.
7., 8. Lift points C and D and fold up. Fold over E and F.
9., 10. Fold bottom half up.
11., 12. Fold G down. Turn over and write race number on frog behind the eyes).

To make the frog jump, press down on the number and release.

Have students line up behind a starting line you have marked on the floor with masking tape, or, if outside, in the schoolyard, with chalk. As each student sets his frog on the starting line, be ready to measure how far it jumps. Record the longest and shortest jumps, and compute the difference between the two. You may wish to allow each frog three jumps, and calculate the average. Students may want to experiment with frogs made of different materials, and record the differences in their jumping abilities.

Notes:

Possible answers to **Frog Life Cycle** activity sheet: **1.** tadpole; tail; store food in my tail **2.** cry, smile, eat, drink a bottle; can't walk yet, go to school, read a book **3.** legs; jump; catch insects; **4.** I can walk, talk, ride a bike, etc.

Possible answers to **Metamorphosis** activity sheet: **1.** will grow into tadpoles, were laid by the mother frog; **2.** tadpoles, have gills, have no legs; **3.** tail; **4.** change, grow, grow legs; **5.** has legs, has eyes near the top of its head, has a bigger mouth; **6.** lungs, grown; **7.** insects; **8.** jump, live on land, have baby frogs, etc.

Frog Life Cycles

Use what you've learned about frogs and their life cycles to fill in the blanks in each box.

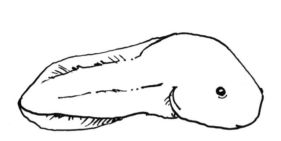

1. I am a _____. I have a _____ instead of legs. I'm different from a grown up frog because I _____

_____

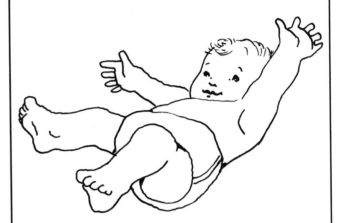

2. I'm a baby. I can _____. I'm different from a grown-up boy or girl because I _____

_____

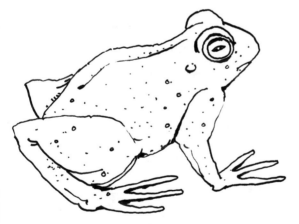

3. I'm a grown-up frog. I have _____. I can _____. I'm different from a baby frog because I _____

_____

(Draw a picture of yourself in this box)

4. I'm a grown up kid. I'm different from a baby because _____

_____

_____

_____

Frog Metamorphosis

Frogs change a lot as they grow. The change is called
Metamorphosis (met-a-**MORE**-fo-sis). Tell about the different
stages of the frog's life in the blank spaces under the pictures.

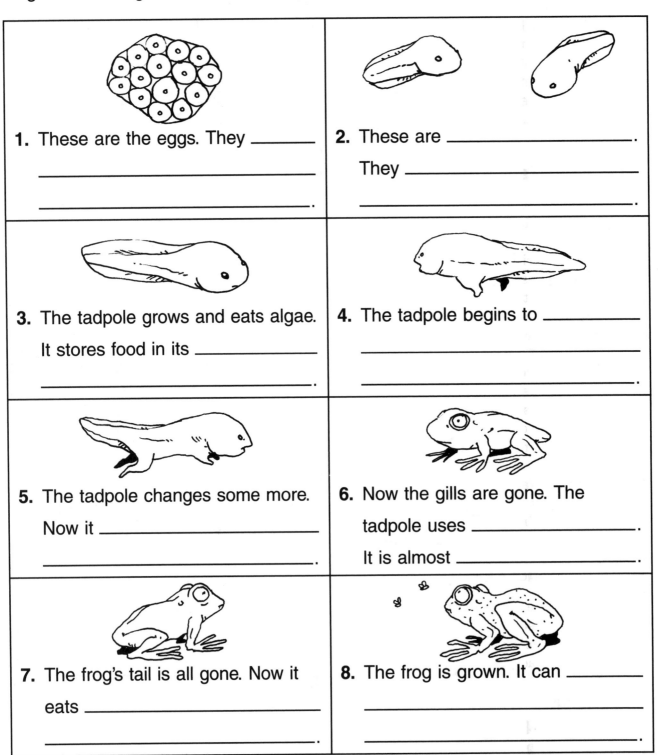

1. These are the eggs. They _____
_____
_____ .

2. These are _____ .
They _____
_____ .

3. The tadpole grows and eats algae.
It stores food in its _____
_____ .

4. The tadpole begins to _____
_____
_____ .

5. The tadpole changes some more.
Now it _____
_____ .

6. Now the gills are gone. The
tadpole uses _____ .
It is almost _____ .

7. The frog's tail is all gone. Now it
eats _____
_____ .

8. The frog is grown. It can _____
_____
_____ .

Detective and Mystery Stories

Most children love detective and mystery stories, but are generally unaware that solving a mystery or just enjoying a mysterious tale utilizes the same thinking skills that are useful in (and out of) school. In this theme unit, recalling details, using logic in problem solving, and planning steps in the completion of a task—all necessary skills when solving mysteries—are emphasized.

Fast Facts

❍ The elements of a mystery or detective story are always the same, whether the author is Ed McBain, writing a "police-procedural" for adults, or the pseudonymous Carolyn Keene (first Edward Stratemeyer, and then his daughter, Harriet Adams), creator of Nancy Drew. They include a crime, witnesses, clues, suspects (with motives and opportunities), and a detective who solves the mystery by logical deduction from clues that have been fairly presented to the reader.

❍ The true mystery story was invented in 1841, with the publication of Edgar Allen Poe's *The Murders in the Rue Morgue*. (Murder, however, is rarely the crime in a children's mystery story.)

❍ The "distinctive detective" was also invented by Poe, with his character Mons. C. Auguste Dupin. However, the most famous of all distinctive, or Great Detectives is, of course, Sherlock Holmes, with his brilliant mind and collection of personality quirks, from his abhorrence of women to his nocturnal violin-playing.

❍ The Holmes-Watson stories also established the sleuth-sidekick model used by many mystery writers in the years since Sir Arthur Conan Doyle first introduced his creations.

Getting Started

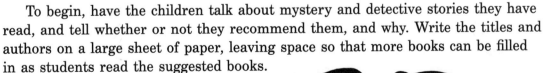

To begin, have the children talk about mystery and detective stories they have read, and tell whether or not they recommend them, and why. Write the titles and authors on a large sheet of paper, leaving space so that more books can be filled in as students read the suggested books.

▼ Reading

Mystery Books

Provide books such as the ones listed below and any others the children may suggest for a classroom library or "Mystery Center."

The Adventure of the Buried Treasure by Nancy McArthur (Scholastic)

The Case of the Double Cross by Crosby Bonsall (Harper & Row)

The Ghost On the Hill by Grace Maccarone (Scholastic)

Gumshoe Goose Private Eye by Mary DeBall Kwitz (Dial)

Nate the Great and the Halloween Hunt by Marjorie Weinman Sharmat (Coward-McCann)

Flatfoot Fox and the Case of the Missing Eye by Eth Clifford (Houghton Mifflin)

The Spy on Third Base by Matt Christopher (Little Brown)

Encyclopedia Brown Carries On (series) by Donald Sobol (Scholastic)

Angie's First Case by Donald Sobol (Scholastic)

Beware! This House Is Haunted Lance Salway (Scholastic)

Secrets in the Attic by Carol Beach York (Scholastic)

Two-Minute Mysteries (series) by Donald Sobol (Scholastic)

Mystery of the Plumed Serpent by Barbara Brenner (Knopf)

Super Sleuth: Twelve Solve-It-Yourself Mysteries by Jackie Vivelo (Putnam's)

▼ Creative Dramatics

Mystery Skits

Have the children form groups of five or six, choose a mystery from the classroom library, and read it aloud to each other over a period of days. When the book is completed and has been discussed, invite the children to work in groups to prepare and present a skit based on the mystery.

▼ Language Arts/Critical Thinking

Listening for Clues/Making Predictions

Take a few days to read aloud a mystery most of your students would be unable to read themselves. One really well-written and researched story is *Mystery of the Plumed Serpent,* listed above. As you read, encourage the children's reactions, and invite them to predict what might happen next at the end of each day's reading. Elicit support for their predictions from the text. Record their predictions in a notebook or on the chalkboard, and during the next day's reading, stop to check on them. Encourage students to see the importance of basing prediction on reasoning from prior knowledge, rather than just guessing or using hunches.

▼ Reading

Making a Book Map

Remind students of the importance of using logic in solving mysteries. Write a book map on the chalkboard, and have the children complete it using one of the mystery books they've read. They can refer to the maps for support when they report to the class on a book and tell why others should read it. Sample book map:

Title: _____

What is the problem to be solved? _____

What are the clues? _____

How did the story end? _____

▼ Language Arts

Elements of Mystery—Writing a Play

Talk about mystery stories in plays, movies, and on television. Select ones that most of the children are familiar with, and help them analyze them in terms of the elements of mystery it contains (see ''Fast Facts''). When the children are thoroughly familiar with the elements and structure, they can write their own mystery play. After the writing, volunteers can read aloud parts of their plays, or put on a full-fledged production.

▼ Science

Fingerprints

Ask everyone to tell anything they know about fingerprints, their use in solving mysteries, and the fact that each person's fingerprints are unique.

Help the children take their own fingerprints, using stamp pads and white paper. Allow them to examine the differences among their fingerprints. Do they think it's true that no two are alike?

▼ Art

Fingerprint Art

Invite the children to make fingerprint art for a mystery book cover. Have them place their prints randomly on a white sheet of paper. Some children may want to make a design using different colored prints. Others may want to incorporate the prints into their drawings of people, animals, cars, etc. The details can be drawn in with crayon or pencil.

▼ Art

Making Disguises

Talk about disguises and how they are used in mysteries. Have the children suggest items that could be used as disguises. Remind the children that altering one's posture, talking with an accent, or making funny noises are all parts of being disguised. Have the children work in groups to plan disguises for themselves. On successive days, each group can leave the classroom for a previously planned area, disguise themselves, and then return, to have classmates guessing. Discussion of the disguises will be fun. Some suggested disguises:

- ○ altered posture
- ○ sunglasses
- ○ yarn wig
- ○ pillow padding
- ○ long coat
- ○ orange-peel teeth

▼ Language Arts

Storytelling

Remind the children that long ago people didn't have books but they told stories, some of which we still tell today.

Point out to the children that many of the books in the classroom library are detective mysteries with clues to solve, often containing humor. Ask the children to suggest other types of mysteries and talk about how the mood and what happens is different in ghost, haunted house, or strange phenomenon mystery stories. Have each group make up a story such as this, going around the circle from person to person. The groups can then share with the class.

Elements of Mystery Checklist

Every mystery must have certain elements; otherwise it wouldn't be mysterious! Use the checklist below to list the elements of mystery you want to include in a mystery story or play you will write yourself.

☐ The Crime   ☐ The Setting

☐ The Suspects   ☐ The Witnesses

☐ The Clues   ☐ The Detective

☐ The Solution

Use the book map below to plan the plot of your mystery.

1.	**TITLE:**	2.	**FIRST,**
	_____		_____
	by		_____
	_____		_____
3.	**THEN,**	4.	**AND FINALLY,**
	_____		_____
	_____		_____
	_____		_____ .

NOW WRITE IT!

Animals of the North Woods

Wolves, bears, and beavers are a but a few of the animals children will meet as they study the habitat of the Superior National Forest in northern Minnesota.

 ## Getting Started

Ask children if they know what a "habitat" is, or if they have ever been to one. Tell them that a habitat is a special place where animals live together naturally, and where the weather and plant life suit their needs.

On a map, point out the area around Lake Superior reaching to the Canadian border. Have children ever been to this part of country? Describe this region as a place in which plants, soil, climate, and animals interact to support each others' continued existence.

Tell students that the climate is warm and humid in the summer, but in the winter it is very cold and snowy, with temperatures that can reach fifty degrees below zero. Is this a place where camels could live? Ask children to support their answers.

Have children brainstorm a list of animals they think might live in this kind of habitat. Write children's suggestions on a large sheet of paper and save it for future reference. As children go through the unit, they can add animal names to the list, or cross out those they feel do not belong.

 ## Language Arts

Writing a Book About Animals

Distribute the activity sheets on page 131 and 132 to the children. Have children read the sheets aloud or silently. After discussing the information, tell children that these sheets can be the first chapter in a book they can call "Animals of the North Woods." Encourage children to illustrate the pages and cut them out to form the pages of a book. They can then go on to research other animal families and model subsequent chapters on the activity sheet. Children can work independently or they can pool their efforts in the form of a class book with contributions from many different authors.

▼ Language Arts and Science

Listening for Information

One of the most interesting animals of the Superior National Forest is the timber wolf. What do children know about wolves? Children may mention wolves that they read about in fairy tales or folktales, or wolves they see in cartoons and films. Are wolves "bad?" Read aloud a book such as *The Call of the Wolves* by Jim Murphy (Scholastic) to children. After the reading, find out if children's ideas about wolves have changed.

▼ Science

Discovering Other Animals In the Habitat

Encourage children to speculate on what other animals may live in the Superior National Forest. List children's suggestions on the chalkboard. Assign small groups of children several animals to research. Encourage children to find interesting facts about food, protective coverings, homes, family groupings, and how they survive the harsh winters. Some good animals to research are:

- ○ moose
- ○ deer
- ○ coyote
- ○ red fox
- ○ northern flying squirrel
- ○ porcupine
- ○ house mouse
- ○ chipmunk
- ○ bat
- ○ snake
- ○ loon
- ○ woodpecker

▼ Social Studies

Finding Information About Black Bears

What do children know about bears? What kinds of bears do they know?

Point out to children that the bears that live in the Superior National Forest are officially named "black bears," but that some of them are brown or even white.

Plan a trip to the library to look for information about black bears. Before you go, make sure children understand how to use tables of contents and indexes. Point out to children that if they wanted to find information about black bears in an encyclopedia, they would look in the encyclopedia index under *bears,* and then under the subheading *black bears.* Encourage children to collect books or magazines containing information on black bears for a classroom library. Back in the classroom, review the material with children. You may wish to supplement their research with the following information:

▼ Art and Social Studies

Thinking About a Wilderness Trip

You may wish to tell children that many campers flock to the Superior National Forest each summer. Ask children if they have ever camped out-of-doors. Have they ever slept in their backyard? Near a lake? In the wilderness? Children who have can share their experiences. Allow them to point out the area on a map, describe what they did, and what animals, birds, or fish they saw.

Locate the book *Three Days On a River in a Red Canoe* by Vera B. Williams (Greenwillow) and read the first seven pages aloud to children. Then skim the book for illustrations, showing children pictures of how the campsite was set up, how the cooking was done, the weather conditions, and the animals that were seen. Allow children to ask questions and comment as you go along.

Tell children that the area of the Superior National Forest closest to the Canadian border is called the Boundary Waters Canoe Area, or BWCA. The BWCA contains over a thousand lakes. Since no motors are allowed on the water, the only means of travel is a canoe.

Invite children to work in groups of three or four to draw a mural depicting a camping trip in a place such as the BWCA. Allow children time to meet and plan their mural. What kinds of scenes do they want to represent?

Provide a sign-up sheet so that groups who want to can read the Vera Williams book, or, alternatively, allow groups to draw their murals using their own experiences or imaginations.

▼ Reading

Reading Books About Animals

Encourage children to read these and other books about animals in the wild.

Animal Books

Animal Families in the Wild: A Read-Aloud Collection of Animal Literature (Crown)

Animal Poems compiled by Anne Carter (Macmillan)

Animal Shelters by Faye Bolton and Esther Cullen (Scholastic)

Animal Moon of the Gray Wolves by Jean Craighead George (HarperCollins)

Bear by John Schoenherr (Putnam's)

Billions of Bats by Miriam Schlein (Lippincott)

Birds, Beasts, and Fishes: A Collection of Busy Beavers by Lydia Dabcovitch (Scholastic)

Come Out Muskrats by Jim Arnosky (Mulberry)

Deer at the Brook by Jim Arnosky (Mulberry)

The Fox by Margaret Lane (Dial) (Others in the series include *The Frog, The Squirrel,* and *The Bear.*)

In the Woods by Ermanno Cristini (Scholastic)

Animals of the North Woods

THE WOLVES

Wolves live in packs with one as the leader. Wolves mate for life. In the spring, babies are born in burrows dug in the ground.

The mother and father wolf go out to hunt deer, moose, and beaver with rest of the pack. An old grandmother or grandfather wolf will take care of the babies during this time.

Animals of the North Woods

Wolves are playful. Mother and father wolves will wrestle and often seem to be hugging. Babies run, chase each other, and jump on older wolves.

People are afraid of wolves, but wolves will not attack a human unless the wolves are trapped or injured. Wolves, hunting in packs, spread out. They howl to communicate. Scientists study the different howling sounds to try to determine what they mean.

The Environment

Children are generally very sensitive to environmental issues. They understand that it is they who will most be affected by environmental neglect. They are concerned that they will inherit a world that is already in serious danger. As you cover the unit, encourage children to follow through with their ideas for independent projects—especially those that involve social or political action.

▶ Getting Started

To begin the unit, ask children what, if any, environmental problems they have come in contact with in their own lives. Have they noticed that the air in their city seems dirty or foul-smelling? Have they been told not to drink water from the tap? Have they been advised not to play within fenced-in areas that contain toxic waste? Then broaden the discussion to include those environmental problems they may have heard about on the news. What has happened to the ozone layer? What about the greenhouse effect? What is acid rain? List these problems and others on the chalkboard. Categorize the issues under the headings Air, Water, and Land.

Saving the Environment

Air	Water	Land
pollution from cars	oil spills	littering
burning garbage	dumping garbage	cutting down trees
people smoking		

▽ Science

Collecting Air Pollution Samples

For this activity, have children work in pairs. Each pair will need the following supplies: an index card, a stick, a small amount of petroleum jelly, masking tape, and waxed paper. Tell children that the purpose of this activity is to collect air samples in various parts of town. On chart paper or the chalkboard, draw a map of your area, or, alternatively, list possible sites that might be good places to collect samples. Write the names of the pairs of children next to each site. When each child has a partner and a site to test, discuss with children the following steps:

1. Write your name and today's date on a card.
2. Tape the card to a stick.
3. Cover the card with petroleum jelly.
4. Wrap it in waxed paper until you get to the test site.
5. When you get to the site, unwrap the card and put the stick into the ground.
6. After 48 hours, remove the stick and the card. Save the card.
7. Repeat the procedure two more times under different weather conditions.

Distribute copies of the activity sheet on page 136, and have children use it to note their observations. Encourage children to compare the air quality under different weather conditions for their site, and then to compare the air quality for the different sites in your area. Ask children what they think causes air to be dirty.

 ## Science

Using an Environmental Checklist at Home

Children can be surprisingly influential at home and in the community when it comes to promoting environmentally sound behavior.

Distribute copies of the activity sheet on page 137 and review it with the children. Encourage children to discuss these or other ideas with family members. Suggest that children hang the checklists on their refrigerators at home and mark off suggestions as they are implemented. After a week or two, have children bring the checklists into class and discuss which of the ideas their families were able to use.

 ## Science and Social Studies

Researching Environmental Hazards

Write these questions—and others children might come up with—on the chalkboard or chart paper:

1. What does recycling mean?
2. Which things in our homes can be recycled? Which things can't?
3. What do we do with our recyclable waste?
4. What does saving electricity have to do with saving the environment?
5. What is the ozone layer and what is harming it?
6. How do food wrappers, soap, pesticides, car oil, PCPs, and salt eventually get into rivers, lakes, and oceans and pollute them?

Have children working in pairs choose one of these questions to research. Before they begin, discuss such sources as indexes and tables of contents, magazines and newspapers, and interviews with parents and community workers. Encourage pairs of children to share their findings with the class in the form of oral presentations, drawings or other graphic aids, and book reports.

▼ Social Studies

Planning and Operating a Paperless Day

Where does paper come from? (trees) Ask children why it is necessary to recycle and save paper. (Trees are a nonrenewable resource; they clean the air, provide a home to thousands of varieties of wildlife, and keep the ecosystem in balance.)

To symbolize the need to save paper, suggest that children have a Paperless Day. Have children in groups discuss ways to conduct classroom activities without using paper. Then have groups submit their suggestions. Write workable ideas on the chalkboard. They might include:

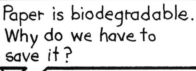

1. Make art objects from old junk and paint.
2. Tell a story instead of writing it.
3. Have an oral spelling test or a spelling bee.
4. Use a computer.
5. Use blocks, cubes, or an abacus for math activities.
6. When bringing lunch to school, use a cloth napkin or small towel instead of a napkin, and a use lunchbox instead of a paper bag.
7. Listen extra hard in class so as not to rely on taking notes.

Hold your Paperless Day. At the end of the day, have children discuss how it worked or didn't work, and how it might have changed their thinking about conserving paper and other resources.

▼ Reading

Books on the Environment

And Still the Turtle Watched by Sheila MacGill-Callahan (Dial)

Cartons, Cans, and Orange Peels: Where Does Our Garbage Go? by Joanna Foster (Clarion)

Earthwatch, Earthsystems, and Ecosystems by Beth Savan (Addison-Wesley)

50 Simple Things Kids Can Do To Save the Earth by The Earthwords Group (Scholastic)

Going Green: A Kid's Handbook to Saving the Planet by Elkington, Hailes, Hill, and Makower (Puffin)

Kids Can Save the Animals: 101 Easy Things to Do by Ingrid Newkirk (Warn)

Mother Earth by Nancy Luenn (Atheneum)

Save the Earth: An Action Handbook for Kids by Betty Miles (Knopf)

Young OWL: The Discovery Magazine for Children by the Naturalist Foundation

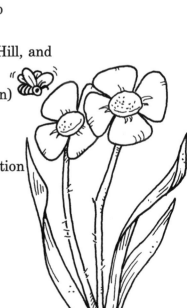

An Air Pollution Observation

by _____ and _____

Site of the experiment _____

DAY 1

Weather: _____

DAY 2

Weather: _____

Observation

What happened to the card? What does that tell you about the cleanliness of the air?

_____

_____

DAY 1

Weather: _____

DAY 2

Weather: _____

Observation

What happened to the card? Was there any difference between the two observations? What was it?

_____

_____

Name: _____

An Environmental Checklist

Put checks next to the words whenever you or someone in your family does one of the following. Add more ideas to the list.

○ Turn off the lights. _____

○ Close the refrigerator. _____

○ Use grocery shopping bags _____

○ Separate bottles and cans _____

○ Use biodegradable soap _____

○ Turn off the water:

leaky faucets _____

brushing teeth _____

washing hands _____

taking quick showers _____

taking a bath _____

_____

_____

_____

_____

_____

_____

Time

Students will enjoy this unit, which will help them tell, measure, and appreciate that most precious commodity—time.

 Getting Started

Begin the unit by asking children to suggest what would happen if there were no such things as clocks and calendars. Encourage the class to brainstorm their ideas. You may wish to use this list to help them get started.

How would I know when my cousin is coming to visit?

If There Were No Clocks

late for school
miss my favorite T.V. show
won't be home on time
lose my paper route
miss lunch
be late for the dentist

If There Were No Calendars

can't plan summer vacation
won't know when the new baby is coming
miss lunch
miss my mom's birthday
miss my birthday
won't know when to expect buds on trees

 Math

Making a Clock

With the increased use of digital watches and clocks, students of all ages may have difficulty telling the time using an analog clock. To help them understand how to read a clock, suggest that they make one of their own.

Provide each child with a circle of oaktag or cardboard. (You can use the cardboard from the back of a writing tablet.) Children can make clock hands from construction paper and one paper fastener, writing in the numbers with crayon or marker. Ask children to draw a frame around their clocks and to decorate them with designs or figures. To help children get ideas for their clock designs, you may wish to show them an illustrated book or catalog featuring different kinds of clocks.

Ask volunteers to demonstrate various times of day on their clocks. You may wish to have children work in pairs, with one partner specifying a particular activity (such as eating dinner) and the other partner displaying the correct time on the clock. You may also try calling out a particular time (such as "a quarter to three") and having children turn the hands of their clocks to the correct time.

Math

Making a Calendar

Ask children if they can remember something that happened in class a month ago. What were they learning about? Did they go on a class trip or put on a play? What was the weather like outside? Guide children to see that a lot can happen in a month's time.

Point out that we use calendars to help us keep track of the days of the week, the weeks of the month, and the months of the year. Then display a large-size calendar for any month. Call out certain days, such as "the third Friday of the month," or "the first day of the last week in the month." Encourage children to identify the correct day.

Give each child a copy of the activity sheet on page 142. Have them make a calendar for the current month and the month to follow. Encourage children to decorate the borders of their calendars with seasonal scenes or images.

After children have completed their work, ask them to look at the two calendars they made. Do both months have the same number of days? How are the months different? How are they the same? Encourage children to take the calendars home and share them with their families.

Ask children to note some important days on the calendars they made. These may be holidays and birthdays, or they may be other days of personal significance. Children can color in the day, decorate it with a picture or image, and write in the name of the day.

 ## Math

Understanding Seconds and Minutes

Ask children if they think they know how long a minute lasts. Using a stop watch or a watch or clock that displays seconds, say "Go!" and have children stand up when they think a minute is up. Were their guesses accurate? Who came the closest?

Tell children that a minutes is made up of sixty seconds. Using your clock or watch, count out the seconds in a minute. Ask children if they know how many minutes there are in an hour. What kinds of things take an hour?

Point out to children that in certain situations a second could make a big difference. Can think of any sports where this might be true? Children may mention football, basketball, hockey, and racing.

 ## Language Arts

Writing a New Version of an Old Story

Locate a version of the Aesop fable "The Tortoise and the Hare." Before reading, tell children that a fable is very short story that teaches a lesson. Read the story aloud and then ask children what lesson was taught and what the fable says about time.

More advanced students may enjoy writing their own fables based on the one by Aesop. As a prewriting activity, ask children to brainstorm ideas for animal characters they could use. Write children's suggestions on the chalkboard. Possible ideas are:

- a bird and an ant race to a place where there are bread crumbs.
- a fly and a mosquito brag about being the first to reach a spider web.
- a bear decides to hibernate in summer instead of winter.
- a tiger is fooled by a tiny field mouse.
- a lazy hen plants her garden just before it snows.

When children have finished the first draft of their fables, suggest that they read them to a partner and have the partner try to identify the moral of the story. After children have revised and proofread their fables, encourage them to read their work to the class.

 Reading

Locating Information

You may find the following books helpful in your classroom discussions about time, clocks, calendars, and seasons.

All Year Long by Richard Scarry (Golden Press)

The Reason for Seasons by Linda Allison (Little, Brown)

This Book is About Time by Marilyn Burns (Little, Brown)

Time in Your Life by Irving Adler (John Day)

Tuesday by David Weisner (Clarion)

Help children form themselves into small groups and give each group a time book. Ask members from each group to peruse their book's table of contents and to identify one section from the book their group would like to read aloud to the class. If an activity is chosen, suggest that the group be responsible for collecting materials and setting up the activity for other class members.

☑ Reading

Listening to Time Travel Stories

Tell children that time travel—the idea that we can step through the present into the past and even into the future—has fired the imaginations of countless writers of science fiction. Ask children if they have ever read a book or seen a movie about time travel. You may wish to locate a copy of one of the following books (or choose one of your own) and read it to the class in segments.

A Wrinkle in Time by Madeline L'Engle (Farrar, Strauss)

Max and Me and the Time Machine by Greer and Ruddick (Harper & Row)

☑ Social Studies

Making Good Use of Time

How can we make the best use of our time? Sometimes it seems as if we never have time to do the things we really want to do, or else we spend a lot of time hanging around being bored. Discuss with the class ideas for making better use of time, such as

○ cutting down on TV watching
○ thinking up projects or activities when there's nothing to do
○ coming up with creative solutions to doing chores, such as doing the less interesting ones early in the day to get them over with
○ planning for special activities with friends or family members

TIME IN ONE DAY OF MY LIFE	
Time	Activity
7:00 to 7:30	Get up- wash face - eat some breakfast - brush my teeth.
7:30 to 8:00	Make my bed - take out garbage do the dishes.
8:00 to 10:00	Lie around
10:00 to 10:15	Talk on the phone
10:15 to 11:30	Ride my bike with Anthony

Suggest that children copy and fill in a time chart—such as the one that has been started here—for a recent Saturday.

Have children share their charts with a partner. Encourage partners to discuss each others' charts and to offer positive suggestions about how each could make better use of his or her time.

Physical Education and Math

Racing With the Clock

As playground activity, have partners time each other as they run. As one partner runs, the other can mark the time by using a watch with a second hand or by counting out the seconds in "mississippis." Challenge children to try for their "personal best" by cutting off as many seconds as possible from their time.

▼ Science

Experimenting with a Sundial

Explain to children that one of the earliest methods of measuring time has been through the use of a sun dial. Although sun dials can be fairly elaborate, they all operate on the same principal—that the sun moves in a predictable way each day. Students may enjoy making and using a simple sun dial that really works.

At exactly 10:00 a.m. on a sunny day, have children put a stake in the ground and observe the shadow it produces. Allow them to check the stake at one- or two-hour intervals. Ask a volunteer to take notes—to draw a picture of each shadow each time it is checked, and to enter the correct time. The next sunny day, ask children to put away all watches and make sure any visible clocks are covered up. At some point during the day, allow children to check the sundial and consult their notes. Challenge children to guess the correct time. Then look at a clock or watch to see how accurate their guesses were.

Time

A Calendar for the Months of _____ and _____

Month: _____

Sun.	Mon.	Tues.	Wed.	Thurs.	Fri.	Sat.

Month: _____

Sun.	Mon.	Tues.	Wed.	Thurs.	Fri.	Sat.

Leonardo Da Vinci

One of the greatest painters of the Italian Renaissance, painter of the "Mona Lisa" and "The Last Supper," Leonardo (as he is usually called) was a genius whose interests and talents led him into the field of science. He was not a true "Renaissance Man," however, having almost no interest in history, literature, or religion. He was an *excellent observer,* who dealt with what the eye could see, rather than with abstractions.

 Fast Facts

○ Leonardo was born in the town of Vinci in 1452. His parents were not married, and he was raised by his father, who apprenticed him at an early age to an artist.

○ Leonardo was left-handed, and his notebooks were written in "mirror-writing," from right to left. It was once believed that he did this to conceal his thoughts, but now, since his writings contain no controversy and can easily be read by anyone with a mirror, it is believed that he wrote this way simply because it was easier for him.

○ He invented the parachute, and devoted a great deal of time to trying to invent a flying machine.

○ By his own count, he autopsied more than 30 corpses for his study of anatomy.

○ He had a child's curiosity and a child's impatience; many of his projects were unfinished. In keeping with his childlike qualities, in one of his notebooks he wrote perfectly serious, detailed instructions for making and launching stink bombs!

 Getting Started

Ask if anyone has heard the name Leonardo Da Vinci. Some children may know he was an artist but others will connect the name with cartoon and other fictional characters.

On a map of Europe, show the country of Italy and invite children to locate the city of Florence. Explain that this was the home of Leonardo Da Vinci, and that he lived from 1452–1519.

This may be a good time to discuss the Renaissance, and to introduce the concept that it was a time of advancement in many fields, from the intellectual, to the political, to the artistic. Leonardo was one of the period's greatest artists.

To help children place Leonardo in history and in relation to themselves, draw a time line on the chalkboard. Start with any event prior to 1500 which you feel

FLORENCE

would have meaning for your students, and extend the line to the year 2000. Have the children speculate on life in the 1400 and 1500s in terms of how people traveled, what they wore, and how they entertained themselves. Help them to see that Leonardo's world was very different from the one we know today.

1492	1776	1929	1984
Columbus sailed	Declaration of Independence	Stock Market crashed	I was born

 Reading

Looking for Information in Words and Pictures

A very good book, even for the youngest of children is *Leonardo Da Vinci the Artist, Inventor, Scientist* by Alice and Martin Provensen (Viking). This and any of the following or other books can be set up for the children in a classroom library:

Da Vinci by Mike Venezia (Children's Press)

Leonardo and the Renaissance by Nathaniel Harris (Bookwright Press)

Leonardo Da Vinci by Ernest Raboff (HarperCollins)

Leonardo Da Vinci by Marshall and Reipamont (Silver Burdett Press)

Leonardo Da Vinci by Kenneth Clark (Children's Press)

A segment in the *World Book Encyclopedia* contains a picture of Leonardo's most famous painting, the "Mona Lisa." (Note: In some reference works, the artist is listed under "L," for Leonardo. In others he can be found under "D," for Da Vinci.)

Depending on the abilities of your students, they may read all or parts of the suggested books, or just look at the illustrations while you read to them. Through the reading, try to emphasize some of the information found in Fast Facts.

 Art

Painting a Portrait

Locate a picture of the "Mona Lisa" and pass it around so that the children can look at it closely. Explain that Leonardo's painting is one of a young wife who actually lived during his time.

Leonardo was able to paint so well because he was an excellent observer. Provide children with pencils, crayons, markers, or paints, and paper, and have them pair up. The members of each pair should take turns observing each other and creating excellently observed portraits. (Use the worksheet on page 147 to exercise students' observation skills.)

 Career Skills

Apprenticeships

Leonardo was an apprentice when he was a young child, and when he grew older he had apprentices of his own. Help your class understand what it means to be an apprentice. Ask if anyone is familiar with the Disney cartoon version of *The Sorcerer's Apprentice*. Many will be. Use this prior knowledge to discuss what it means to be an "apprentice," and how apprentices are similar to and different from students, like those in your class. (*Apprentices* are young people who are in training to enter a trade, and who usually learn only the skills related to that trade. *Students* receive a more general education, and their career plans are not yet determined. Union locals in your area may be willing to provide information on apprenticeship programs that you can use.) Some of your students may have parents who are or were apprentices, and they may be willing to come to school to discuss their experiences with your class.

Invite children to think of jobs they'd like to have when they grow up. Ask them to describe what they think it would be like to be an apprentice in that field.

▼ Penmanship

Mirror Writing

Invite students to try "Mirror Writing" It's not terribly difficult, but it does take practice. In mirror writing, letters are formed backwards, and the lines on the page are written from right to left. In order to read the writing, students need a straight-edged hand mirror (the cheap kind available in variety stores is fine), which they hold upright along the edge of the paper (see diagram).

▼ Technology

Flying Machines

In honor of Leonardo's efforts to invent a flying machine, hold a paper airplane contest in your classroom to provide a variety of cross-curricular experiences for your students.

Invite students to design and create paper airplanes that will perform well in any or all of three categories: distance, time aloft, and aerobatics. In order to encourage creative thinking and experimentation, don't use the word "airplane" when describing the project: Tell students that they are to design paper *objects* that will fly. Most students will create the familiar paper "dart" that has been the bane of schoolteachers throughout time. However, try to get them away from thinking traditionally and move them toward developing designs based on the function the object is to perform, and not some preconceived idea of what it should look like.

Tell students they may use scissors, glue, and paper, but no tape, staples or clips. They can bend, fold or cut their flying machines, or use glue to attach flaps, longer wings, etc. Take the class to the gym or auditorium to fly their creations. Time the flights with a stopwatch, and use a tape measure to record distance. Make the activity as fun or as formal as you want, and encourage students to analyze the different designs and the results they produce.

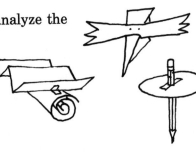

▼ Extension activities:

○ **Language Arts**—write a report about the contest for the school newspaper, or write a script for a radio broadcast over the school public address system telling about the contest and its results. Winners can be interviewed, etc.

○ **Reading**—read to students from *The Great International Paper Airplane Book* by Jerry Mander, George Dippel, and Howard Gossage (Simon and Schuster). This book contains patterns for paper airplanes that you can share with your class.

○ **Math**—allow students three attempts to fly each entry, average the distance and time aloft of each; graph results; convert distances in feet to meters, etc.

○ **Art**—planes can be decorated with markers, crayons, paints, etc.

○ **Science**—think about energy sources. Who or what provided the energy for the paper airplanes? (The students!) Are there other forms of transportation that are "people powered"?

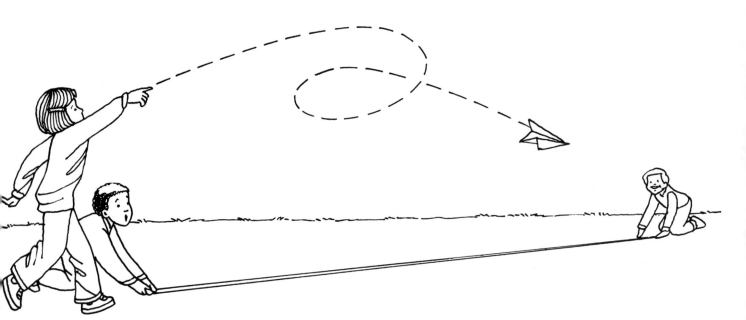

Being an Excellent Observer

Leonardo was an "excellent observer," which means he looked very carefully at things. Look very carefully at the picture below to find the hidden items.

mirror writing	parachute	paint brush
palette	flying machine	map of Italy

Tall Tales

A tall tale is a kind of folktale; that is, a story that develops in a certain region of the world and is passed down from generation to generation. A tall tale usually begins somewhat realistically and then spins off into the realm of the fantastic, the absurd, or the wildly improbable, using exaggerated details that delight and amuse listeners of all ages.

 ## Getting Started

Write the word *exaggeration* on the chalkboard and ask children to tell what they think it means. Can they give an example of exaggeration? How can exaggeration be used in storytelling? Tell children the following tall tale, or choose another with which you are familiar.

Way, way back, a long time ago, I was living out on a farm raising chickens with nothing but a pet spider, Spidie, for company. Now Spidie was so little it took three people to see him and I wasn't so big myself, as you can see. Well anyway, one day two crooks came out to my farm to steal my chickens. Now I forgot to tell you Spidie could run as fast as a jet plane can fly. He ran after those crooks and was back before he started. Not only that, while he was running he stung one crook with one of his stingers. The crook stopped in one minute. Then Spidie stung the other with another stinger. This time, the crook lasted two seconds before stopping. Spidie and I live in Hollywood now. We're making movies with Arnold Yulenshpeeger.

Ask children to mention all the instances of exaggeration they can remember. Write their ideas on the chalkboard. Which ones did they like best? Why was this story a tall tale?

Language Arts

Creating Growing Fox Tales

Set up a bulletin board displaying a cut-out outline of a fox with a short tail. Encourage children to write their own tall tales and mount them on the fox's tail. Have them watch the fox's tail growing longer as tall tales accumulate.

Social Studies

Finding Out About "Big Paul"

Use a map or globe to point out regions of the United States that gave rise to some of the most popular American tall tales. Point out that many of these stories centered on "bigness" because America seemed so big to the pioneers and immigrants. Show students the state of Texas and tell them that this large state is the place where tales of Pecos Bill originated. (Children may remember that Pecos Bill rode on a cyclone.) Encourage children to locate the Great Lakes and tell them that according to legend, the lakes were created by Paul Bunyan. Children may know that "Big Paul" had a blue ox named Babe, who measured forty-two ax handles between the eyes.

Tell or read children a Paul Bunyan tale. A good choice is *Paul Bunyan* by Steven Kellogg (Morrow).

 Storytelling

Writing Original "Big Paul" Tales

Many tall tales were first told as people sat around campfires at night exchanging stories. Allow children to form groups of four or five. Have group members sit in a circle and collaborate on an original "Big Paul" story. Encourage one group member to begin the story, and others in turn to continue until the end. Remind children to use exaggeration and fantasy. When the story is completed, a volunteer from each group can tell the group's tale to the class, or, alternately, the group can try to write their story down.

 Math

Figuring Out "Bigness"

Tell people that according to legend, Paul Bunyan was fifty times taller than other children by the time he was eight years old. Let's say an eight year old is four feet tall. Ask children to use a ruler, piece of string, or other measure to figure out how big he was. Would he fit in the room?

Science and Art

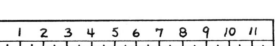

Researching Lumbering, Then and Now

Tell children that Paul Bunyan stories originated in the lumber camps of the Midwest. Ask children to look in an encyclopedia or other reference work to find out how it was to live and work in lumber camps during the late nineteenth century. Who worked in lumber camps? Was it dangerous? Why did people work in this industry? Why do you think this tale was told? Children might also be curious to find out how the lumber industry has changed over the years. Have volunteers share their findings with the class.

▼ Reading

Reading Tall Tale Books

American Tall Tales by Stoutenburg (Viking)

Jack and the Whoopee Wind by Calhoun (Morrow)

Ol' Paul by Rounds (Holiday House)

Pecos Bill by Kellogg (Morrow)

Tall Tales from the High Hills by Credle (Thomas Nelson)

Whoppers, Tall Tales, and Other Lies by Schwartz (Lippincott)

▼ Creative Dramatics

Acting Out Tall Tales

Suggest that children working in small groups find a tall tale to act out. Some members of the group can take the roles of the characters, and one group member can function as the story's narrator. Encourage children to use their imaginations. They may choose to "act out" inanimate objects, to further exaggerate the story, or to change it or add new characters.

▼ Social Studies

Learning About Baron von Munchausen

Encourage children to be library detectives. Their assignment: Find out everything they can about Baron von Munchausen! Who was he? What did he do?

You may already know that Baron von Munchausen was actually a German adventurer who served in the Russian army during the eighteenth century. His wildly exaggerated accounts of his war experiences are said to be the model for all tall tales.

After children have found the answer to your questions, suggest that they look for the film *The Adventures of Baron von Munchausen* in their local video store.

▼ Writing and Art

Taking a Tall Tale Survey

As a culminating activity, encourage children to write a tall tale with themselves as the main character—possibly disguised as a "larger-than-life" hero or heroine or powerful animal.

Suggest that students use the activity sheet on page 151 to help them in the prewriting stage. They can then go on to write their drafts, revisions, and final version.

Children may use their own ideas, or they may begin their stories with one of the following opening sentences:

○ Being trapped by a coyote can be interesting.
○ They call me Paulina Bunyan!
○ I didn't know eating grass could turn you into a wolf.

Completed tales can be copied onto very, very long and narrow paper (try notebook paper cut in half and taped end-to-end). Display children's work on a wall or bulletin board.

Name: _____

My Very Own Personal, Up-To-Date and Absolutely True—Sort Of—Tall Tale

Give yourself this quiz.
Then use it to write or tell a tall tale.

1. Am I a person or an animal? _____

2. How big am I? _____

3. How strong am I? _____

4. What things did I make all by myself?

   _____   _____

   _____   _____

5. Here are some exaggerated things I saw. I can add more.

   I saw:
   A wind so strong it blew the rabbits out of their holes.
   A fly so big it picked up a bear.

   _____

   _____

   _____

Here's what happens in my story:

The beginning _____

_____

The middle _____

_____

The end _____

_____

_____

_____

_____

Our Neighbors to the North and South— Canada and Mexico

Students may be surprised to learn that "America" doesn't just refer to the United States. Use this unit to help children learn more about our neighbors on the continent of North America.

 ## Fast Facts—Canada

○ Canada covers half the territory on the continent of North America and is comprised of ten provinces and two territories.

○ With the dissolution of the Soviet Union, Canada became the largest country in the world.

○ Eric the Red, a Norwegian explorer, is credited with discovering Canada in 985 A.D.

○ The French, in 1605, were the first Europeans to settle in Canada. Quebec is still populated by French-speaking people.

○ In 1783 settlers from England came, as well as English loyalists and free blacks from the American colonies. England's queen is still identified with Canada although she holds no true authority there.

○ The United States and Canada share the largest undefended border in the world, and the two country's governments and industry work together.

 ## Fast Facts—Mexico

○ Mexico shares a 2,000 mile border with the United States.

○ Mexico is a land of deserts, mountains, swampy areas and jungles and was first settled by Native Americans.

○ Most of Mexico's people are farmers, but many others work in factories and offices.

○ Mexicans are among the earliest immigrants to the United States, with some arriving in the early 1600's.

○ Mexico has a rich culture combining influences of Spain with the Mayan and Aztec civilizations.

 ## Getting Started

Help the children locate Canada and Mexico on a wall map. Have students explain why we call Canada "Our Neighbor to the North" and Mexico "Our

Neighbor to the South. " Ask children who have visited these places to bring in photographs recounting their trips, and have the children use the photos to help describe their experiences to the rest of the class. Invite children to bring in Mexican and Canadian souvenirs and artifacts to display for the group.

Reading

Books About Canada and Mexico

Canada . . . in Pictures (Lerner)

Canada by Susan Williams (Franklin Watts)

Land and People of Canada by Andrew Malcolm (Harper Collins)

Mexico by Sam and Beryl Epstein (Franklin Watts)

We Live in Mexico by Carlos Somonte (Bookwright Press)

Map Skills

Learning About Our Canadian Neighbors

List the names of the Canadian provinces and territories on a large sheet of paper and help the children read them. From east to west, they are:

1. Newfoundland
2. Prince Edward Island
3. Nova Scotia
4. New Brunswick
5. Quebec
6. Ontario
7. Manitoba
8. Saskatchewan
9. Alberta
10. British Columbia
11. The Yukon
12. The Northwest Territories

Using a topographical map of North America, have the children take turns pointing out Canada's provinces and territories and the physical terrain of each. On the activity sheet on page 156, have the children copy the names of the provinces and territories. As children learn more about Canada's cities, resources and waterways, children may want to add such information to their maps. Ask children how the terrain of the land and the location of the water might affect where and how people live in Canada.

Map Skills

Learning About Our Mexican Neighbors

Have the children find Mexico on a topographical map and have them use the map key to find areas with low and wet lands, high and arid plateaus and three-mile high mountains. Then have the children point out the continents of North and South America, and the positions of Canada, the United States, and Mexico. Ask them to replicate the information in the map on the activity sheet on page 157. They may also fill in the names of cities, ruins, and products.

▽ Social Studies

Invite a Mexican Visitor

Ask a native Mexican or anyone who has toured Mexico to visit your class and talk about life in Mexico. Prepare a list of questions concerning some of the following:

○ the capital and other cities of Mexico
○ what is made and grown there
○ the principal tourist areas and what they have to offer
○ life in small villages
○ the language

If your visitor speaks Spanish, have him or her offer your class an easy Spanish lesson. Generate a list of familiar words and phrases in both Spanish and English. Later, use the list to create illustrated bilingual dictionaries.

Variation: Repeat this activity by inviting a native Canadian to your class.

▽ Language Arts

Learning Words in Spanish and French

Remind students that while many of our neighbors to the north and south speak English, Spanish is the first language in Mexico and French the standard language in the Canadian Province of Quebec.

Share bilingual picture books such as *El Sombrero Del Tio Nacho* by Harriet Rohmer (Children's Press), in Spanish and English and *Babar's French Lessons* by Laurent De Brunhoff (Random House).

▽ Social Studies

"Good Neighbors" Bulletin Board

Cover a bulletin board with craft paper and print the heading: "Good Neighbors." Use markers to divide the display into three equal columns and label as shown in the diagram below. The purpose of the display is to highlight the similarities among Canada, the United States, and Mexico. During the course of the unit, have the children add or dictate information and supply drawings or paintings to illustrate.

Good Neighbors

	Canada	U.S.	Mexico
Size			
Flag			
Language(s)			
Climate	cool	temperate	warm
Favorite Foods			

▽ Social Studies

Pack Your Bags

Have children use copies of the activities on pages 156 and 157 to help children imagine they are planning a trip to Mexico or to Canada. Begin by contacting a travel agency in order to secure travel brochures featuring several possible destinations within each region. In order to decide on a destination, students should research and then use activity page 159 to log and compare information about transportation, climate, sights to see, activities, accomodations and food available at each location. (To research transportation costs, students could estimate the mileage from their homes to desired locations in Canada or Mexico, and then multiply that number by the cost of gasoline per gallon. Or, they could contact airlines and railways to compare ticket fares.)

To further help with their decision-making (and in order to help students prepare for the trip once a destination has been chosen), students may use the suitcase pictured on activity page 158 to "pack" clothing and sundry items they would need to have a successful trip.

Art

Making Paper Mache Bowls

Through their studies of Mexico and Canada, the children will learn about Mexican pottery and the English bone china common to Canada (because of its affiliation with England).

1. Blow up a balloon and tie it closed.
2. Fold newspaper to make a strip of two or three layers. The strip should be long enough to encircle the balloon in order to form a stand to hold it up.
3. Cover the lower half of the balloon with paper strips dipped in flour and water. Two or three layers are needed to form the thickness of the bowl.
4. Set the "bowl," with the balloon intact, into the paper circle.
5. Attach the "bowl" to the strip with more paper mache strips.
6. Let everything dry over night.
7. Break the balloon and gently pull it out.
8. Paint the bowls with one solid color and then decorate to resemble Canadian or Mexican pottery designs.

Canadian Map

Answer the questions by writing or drawing right on the map.
1. Write N for north, S for south, E for east, and W for west
   to show directions.
2. Write the names of the provinces and territories.
3. Write the names of the big cities and mountain ranges.
4. Draw tiny pictures in each section to tell more about Canada.

Name: _____

Mexican Map

Answer the questions by writing or drawing right on the map.

1. Write N for north, S for south, E for east, and W for west to show directions.
2. Choose three colors for the map key. One color should be for low, wet lands, another for high, arid plateaus, and a third for three-mile-high mountains.
3. Color in the map using your key.
4. Write names of famous cities and places.
5. Draw tiny pictures to tell more about Mexico.

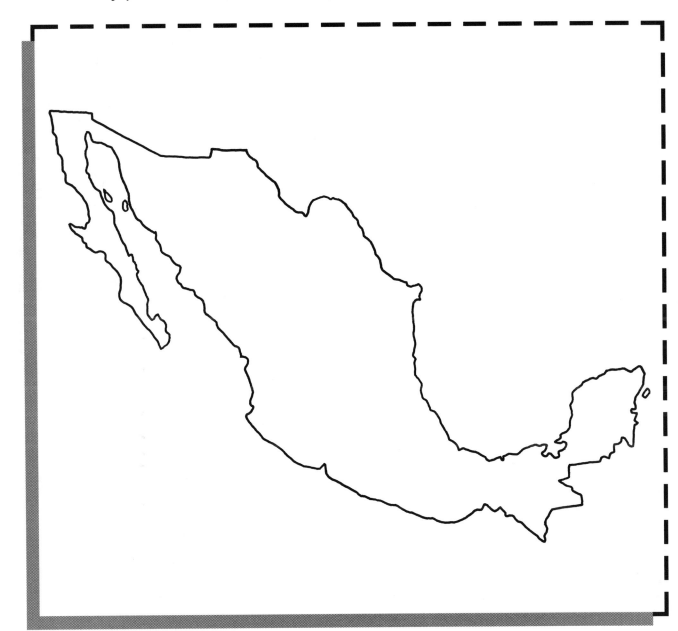

Pack Your Bags!

In the suitcase, draw or glue pictures showing what you will need for your trip to Canada or Mexico! *Bon voyage! Hasta luego!*

Our Neighbors to the North and South

Destination	Type of Transportation	Cost of Transportation	Climate	Sights to See	Activities	Accomodation

Summer Vacation

No matter how much they love school, most children look forward to summer vacation. Take the opportunity to talk about and plan summer months so that this may be their best vacation yet.

 Getting Started

Title a bulletin board "Summer's Coming." Ask the children what kinds of pictures and related information they might put up on the board to remind them of summer fun. Encourage them to add to the bulletin board in the last few weeks of school and to share any summer plans and projects they are looking forward to. Use the activity sheet on page 164 to get them started.

Language Arts

Listening and Writing

To help children begin to experience summer, provide some summer fun for all five of the senses.

Sight—Invite children to bring in photographs illustrating how they spent prior summers. Students may also clip pictures from magazines or travel brochures that depict their ideal summer pastimes.

Hearing—Have children brainstorm a list of summer hangouts and hideaways such as amusement parks, city sidewalks, the beach, the backyard, the park, the mountains, etc. As you describe the details of each spot, invite the children to close their eyes and imagine they are at each one. Help children to concentrate especially on the sounds common to each location. Record these sounds on chart paper or the blackboard.

Summer Sounds

rollercoaster: screams

at the beach: seagulls and waves

in the mountains: crickets!

Touch—Have children bring to school personal possessions that remind them of summer. Some suggestions could include sunglasses, a bottle of sunscreen, a sand pail and shovel, a beach hat, sandals, sea shells, rocks, etc. Place items one at a time into a box or bag and have children take turns trying to guess each other's items by touch alone.

Taste and Smell—Serve up some traditional summer treats such as watermelon, lemonade or frozen fruit juice pops. Or, consider planning a full-blown end-of-the-year summer picnic complete with baked beans, hot-dogs, buns, and brownies. Either way, ask students to describe how the smell and taste of the food helps them to remember special summer moments.

After providing the children with some of the above concrete sensory experiences, have the children work in pairs to record summertime nouns they associate with each of the five senses. Use chart paper to synthesize each list into one master list that may be posted in the writing corner for students to incorporate into their own reflections of summer.

▼ Math

Creating a Week-at-a-Peek Calendar

Talk about calendars and their uses. Explain the concept of "week-at-a-peek" and give each child three copies of the activity sheet on page 163.

Depending on your class, students may work alone, in groups, or with you to fill in the days of the week and the names of each summer month. After reviewing samples of calendar pads featuring decorative scenes mounted above calendar pages, encourage children to draw or paint summer scenes for their own calendars. These scenes may be mounted on the top half of a large piece of construction paper or oaktag. Calendar pages may then be stacked in order and stapled beneath the mounted pictures.

On a separate day, brainstorm activity ideas to log into each day of the summer calendars, such as:

○ plans with friends
○ plans with family
○ something special to learn or practice (dancing, roller skating, writing a book, building a toy, writing letters, etc.)
○ books to read
○ helping mom, dad, grandparents, brothers, sisters, cousins, friends, neighbors

Encourage students to exchange ideas regarding calendar activities. Present calendars to the children to keep on the last day of school.

▼ Science

Making a Windowsill Garden

Many gardening books are now available to help young children develop green thumbs. These books teach youngsters how to grow plants from potatoes, avocado pits, carrot tops, grass seed, plant cuttings, fruit seeds, bean sprouts, herbs, etc. Many of these plants can be started in school and transported home for replanting.

Encourage the children to recycle plastic food containers into sprouting containers and plant pots. Containers printed with lettering or advertisements may be wrapped in tissue or covered in construction paper. Plain containers may be decorated with permanent opaque "paint markers" available in art supply stores.

▼ Reading

Making Lists

In groups, the children can use the bulletin boards and walls to post lists of recommended summer reading. Some groups may provide story suggestions while others can list non-fiction titles including books of jokes and riddles, craft and drawing books, collections of science experiments, how-to books featuring things to build, games to play and songs to learn.

Some non-fiction titles you'll want children to know about include:

Don't Just Sit There: 50 Ways to Have a Nickelodeon Day by Daniella Burr, (Grosset & Dunlap)

Easy-to-Make Water Toys That Really Work by Mary and Dewey Blocksma (Simon & Schuster)

Drawing America by Don Bolognese and Elaine Raphael (Scholastic)

Discovering Science Secrets by Sandra Markle (Scholastic)

I Am Curious About Numbers: A Curious George Activity Book (Scholastic)

I Can Draw People by Gill Spiers (Simon & Schuster)

Kids' America by Steven Caney (Workman)

Kids' Big Book of Games edited by Karen Anderson (Workman)

Sand Creatures and Castles: How to Build Them by Bob and Pat Reed (Holt, Rinehart and Winston)

Secret Spaces Imaginary Places: Creating Your Own Worlds for Play by Elin McCoy (Macmillan)

Super Summer Fun edited by Laima Dingwall and Annabel Slaight (OWL Magazine/Golden Press Book)

 ## Health and Safety

Talking about Summer Safety

Hold a safety discussion that emphasizes the home and the special outdoor conditions of your area. The children will have many suggestions (which you may list on the Summer's Coming bulletin board) such as:

○ using stoves, knives, and scissors with the help of grown-ups
○ following parents' directions about what not to touch in and out of the house
○ swimming and hiking with supervision
○ paying attention in traffic

Give each child a large sheet of construction paper and have them print the words: HAVE A SAFE SUMMER. They can illustrate, give a short speech on what their picture means, and take the poster home to hang it up in a prominent place.

 ## Language Arts

Making An Autograph Book

Create an autograph book for each student by cutting a supply of construction paper in half and stapling the halves together. Students may use books to record phone numbers, funny notes, jokes, and good wishes for the summer. Allow a few minutes each day for students to record messages in each other's books.

A Week at a Peek

Make a one-week calendar. Write the name of the month on top. Write the days of the week from Sunday to Saturday. Use the calendar to plan your summer.

Month: _____

One Week in My Summer Life

From Sunday ___ To Saturday ___	Sunday	Monday	Tuesday	Wednesday	Thursday	Friday	Saturday

Summer Vacation

Think of the most wonderful things you can about what you will do this summer. Then write a few rhyming lines or a whole story on other paper telling about them. Draw a picture to illustrate your writing. Read the story to your family or your best friend.

In Summertime

In Summertime, _____

_____

_____

_____

_____

_____